FAST PASS FOR THE TOEIC® L&R TEST

Revised Edition

Ritsuko Uenaka | Seiko Korechika

Australia • Brazil • Mexico • Singapore • United Kingdom • United States

PAST PASS FOR THE TOEIC® L&R TEST, Revised Edition

Ritsuko Uenaka / Seiko Korechika

© 2019 Cengage Learning K.K.

ALL RIGHTS RESERVED. No part of this work covered by the copyright herein may be reproduced, transmitted, stored, or used in any form or by any means—graphic, electronic, or mechanical, including but not limited to photocopying, recording, scanning, digitizing, taping, Web distribution, information networks, or information storage and retrieval systems—without the prior written permission of the publisher.

"National Geographic", "National Geographic Society" and the Yellow Border Design are registered trademarks of the National Geographic Society ® Marcas Registradas

The *TOEIC*® Listening and Reading Test Directions (pages 12–14, 16, 17, 19, and 20):
Copyright © 2015 Educational Testing Service. *TOEIC*® Listening and Reading Test Directions are reprinted by permission of Educational Testing Service, the copyright owner. All other information contained within this publication is provided by Cengage Learning K.K. and no endorsement of any kind by Educational Testing Service should be inferred.

Photo Credits:
front cover: © BILL HATCHER/National Geographic Creative; 12 © Educational Testing Center; 13 (t) © Comstock Images/ Stockbyte/Getty Images, (b) © spyarm/iStock.com; 24 © lisapics/iStock.com; 25 © Michael Blann/DigitalVision/Getty Images; 26 (l) © monkeybusinessimages/iStock.com, (r) Comstock Images/Stockbyte/Getty Images, (b) © Naddiya /iStock.com; 29 © Todd Warnock/Lifesize/Thinkstock; 32 © Little_Airplane/iStock.com; 34 © ArtMarie/iStock.com; 36 © Sergio Bellott/iStock.com; 39 © martinedoucet/iStock.com; 44 © Alphotographic/iStock.com; 49 © Creatas/ Thinkstock; 54 © bmcent1/iStock.com; 56 © Stefan Ilic/iStock.com; 59 © LuckyBusiness/iStock.com; 64 © PeopleImages/iStock.com; 65 © monkeybusinessimages/iStock.com; 66 (l) © Antonio_Diaz/iStock.com, (r) © 97/iStock.com, (b) © CSA-Images/iStock.com; 69 © Digital Vision/Digital Vision/Getty Images; 74 ©YinYang/iStock.com; 76 © Anthonycz/iStock.com; 79 © Pete saloutos/UpperCut Images/Getty Images; 84 © PeopleImages/iStock.com; 86 © Owat Tasai/iStock.com; 89 © iStockphoto/Thinkstock; 94 © olm26250/iStock.com; 99 © Ron Chapple Studios/Thinkstock; 104 © bee32/iStock.com; 105 © DigitalVision/DigitalVision/Getty Images; 106 (l) © DragonImages/iStock.com, (r) © g-stockstudio/iStock.com, (b) © RedlineVector/iStock.com; 109 © LightFieldStudios/iStock.com; 114 © Cimmerian/iStock.com; 116 © FrankRamspott/iStock.com; 119 © jacoblund/iStock.com; 124 © Robert Daly iStock.com; 126 © Murata Yuki/iStock.com; 129 © Hemera/Thinkstock; 134 © Nonwarit/iStock.com; 136 © CSA-Archive/iStock.com; 139 © Hemera/Thinkstock

For permission to use material from this textbook or product, e-mail to **eltjapan@cengage.com**

ISBN: 978-4-86312-350-2

National Geographic Learning | Cengage Learning K.K.
No. 2 Funato Building 5th Floor
1-11-11 Kudankita, Chiyoda-ku
Tokyo 102-0073
Japan

Tel: 03-3511-4392
Fax: 03-3511-4391

はじめに

　本書は *TOEIC*® L&R テストの更なるスコアアップを求める中級レベルの学習者を対象とした総合テキストです。

　TOEIC® テストは 2016 年 5 月に問題形式に一部変更が加えられ、正式名称も *TOEIC*® Listening & Reading Test に変わりました。本書は『FAST PASS FOR THE TOEIC® TEST』の改訂版で、2016 年 5 月から導入された新形式問題に対応しています。Part 3 の 3 名の会話を聞いて答える問題、Part 3 及び Part 4 の図表を伴う問題、Part 6 の文選択問題、Part 7 のオンラインチャットの問題、3 つの文書の問題などの新しい問題形式の追加、また旧問題の変更をしています。

　本書は全 12 ユニットで構成されており、巻頭に Pre-test（50 問：約 35 分）を掲載しています。また、Teacher's Manual（教授用書）には Post-test（50 問：約 35 分）、及び MINI TOEIC L&R TEST の Listening Section のスクリプトを収録しています。Pre-test は学習前の実力診断に、Post-test は学習効果の診断に利用してください。なお、各ユニットの後半にはリスニング、リーディングすべてのパートの練習問題に取り組む MINI TOEIC L&R TEST（約 20 分）を配しており、スコア記録表を巻末に収めています。MINI TOEIC L&R TEST は各ユニットの学習内容の定着と、実際の *TOEIC*® L&R テストの問題形式に慣れるように工夫されています。

　各ユニットは、《料理、食事》《雇用、就職》などテーマ別に構成されるとともに、リスニングおよびリーディングセクションの各パートの特徴をとらえた攻略法を収めています。思うように得点が伸びずに学習の壁にぶつかっている学習者、特にビジネス関係の内容理解に苦しんでいる学習者のために、本書では後半の 6 つのユニットでビジネス関連テーマを扱い、集中的かつ効果的に理解の深層化を図っています。

　ユニットの前半では、リスニング能力アップのための会話の聞き取りや、リーディング能力アップのための速読・文法解説などとともに exercise に取り組み、後半では MINI TOEIC L&R TEST で *TOEIC*® L&R テストの練習問題に挑戦し、形式に慣れるよう構成しています。

　本書が *TOEIC*® L&R テスト受験対策に向けて、学習者のレベルアップと、総合的な英語力の向上に大いに役立つことを願っています。

　最後に本書の編集にご尽力いただいたナショナルジオグラフィック ラーニングの吉田剛氏、販売にご奔走いただいた山本哲也氏に心から感謝いたします。また、本書刊行にあたり忍耐強くご支援いただいた同社の皆様に深くお礼を申し上げます。

上仲律子・是近成子

Contents 目次

TOEIC® Listening & Reading Test について 6
本書の構成と効果的な使い方 8
Pre-test（50問）.. 12
MINI TOEIC L&R TEST スコア記録表／自己分析表 144, 145
解答用紙（Pre-test用、Post-test用）............................ 147, 149

Unit	Topic	Tips	
1	**Food & Restaurant** 料理、食事	Part 1	瞬時に適切な描写文を予想する
2	**Entertainment** 娯楽、芸術	Part 2	質問文の最初の語をとらえる
3	**Travel** 旅行、観光	Part 3	3人の会話と話し手の意図を問う設問
4	**Sports & Health** スポーツ、健康	Part 4	ざっくばらんな表現や音の脱落などに注意する
5	**Purchasing** 買い物、注文	Part 1	被写体の配置をすばやくとらえる
6	**Housing & Accommodations** 住宅・不動産、宿泊施設	Part 2	Yes/No疑問文は内容をよく理解する
7	**Office Work (1)** 日常業務、販売	Part 3	連結音に耳を慣らしておく
8	**Office Work (2)** クレーム処理、出荷	Part 4	説明文が流れる前に図を確認し、質問文を速読する
9	**Employment** 雇用、就職	Part 1	周りの状況をすばやくチェックする
10	**Lectures & Presentations** 講演、発表	Part 2	意外な応答に慣れる
11	**Business Affairs (1)** 交渉、契約	Part 3	選択肢から会話の内容を予想する
12	**Business Affairs (2)** 市場調査、売り込み	Part 4	頻出ジャンルの質問パターンに慣れる

		Grammar Points	Page
Part 5	問題のタイプを見分ける	名詞	24
Part 6	文の構造をしっかり把握する・文選択問題	代名詞	34
Part 7	スマホやパソコンでのインターネット会話に慣れよう	助動詞	44
Part 5	語と語の意味の結びつきに注目する	形容詞	54
Part 6	主語と述語動詞をしっかり把握する	時制（1）現在進行形	64
Part 7	5W1Hに注目する・文挿入問題	時制（2）過去形・現在完了形	74
Part 5	句動詞を身につける	動名詞と不定詞	84
Part 6	空所を含む文の前後の文に注目する	似た意味をもつ前置詞	94
Part 7	未知語にとらわれないで読み進める・質問形式に慣れる	注意すべき比較表現	104
Part 5	接頭辞と接尾辞をマスターして語彙を増やす	仮定法	114
Part 7	ダブルパッセージの問題に慣れる	関係詞	124
Part 7	記入用紙の書式に慣れる	接続詞	134

TOEIC® Listening & Reading Test について

　TOEIC® とは Test of English for International Communication の略称で、英語によるコミュニケーション能力を評価するテストです。現在、世界約 160 カ国で実施されており、日本での公開テストと IP テストを合わせた受験者数は 2015 年度には 250 万人を超えました。評価は合格・不合格ではなく、Listening が 5 点〜495 点、Reading が 5 点〜495 点、合計 10 点〜990 点のスコアで評価されます。

　社会のグローバル化に伴い、国際社会に対応できる人材が必要とされています。国際的に展開する企業では採用や昇進の際に TOEIC® L&R テストのスコアを要件とするところが増えており、実践的な英語コミュニケーション能力のある人材が求められています。調査によると、「社員採用時に TOEIC® L&R テストのスコアを参考にする（将来は参考にしたい）」と回答した企業は 228 社のうち 78.4% に達しており、新入社員に期待する TOEIC® L&R テストのスコアは平均で約 565 点となっています。
　大学生と新入社員の平均スコアは次の表のとおりです。

	公開テスト	IP テスト
大学生	565 （L: 311　R: 255）	449 （L: 253　R: 196）
短大生	473 （L: 279　R: 194）	411 （L: 249　R: 162）
新入社員	—	485 （L: 262　R: 222）

（資料：一般財団法人 国際ビジネスコミュニケーション協会発行『TOEIC® Program DATA & ANALYSIS 2018』）

TOEIC® Listening & Reading Test の構成と出題形式

　TOEIC® Listening & Reading Test は次の表のような構成になっています。各セクション 100 問ずつ、計 200 問を約 2 時間にわたって行います。休憩時間はありません。

Listening　100 問／約 45 分間	Reading　100 問／75 分間
Part 1　　6 問：写真描写問題　　4 択	Part 5　　30 問：短文穴埋め問題　　4 択
Part 2　 25 問：応答問題　　　　3 択	Part 6　　16 問：長文穴埋め問題　　4 択
Part 3　 39 問：会話問題　　　　4 択	Part 7　　54 問：読解問題　　　　　4 択
Part 4　 30 問：説明文問題　　　4 択	

TOEIC® Listening & Reading Test では、解答方法の指示や各パートの説明等がすべて英文で提示されます。各パートの説明（Directions）は、本書の Pre-test に記載しています。

● **Part 1　写真描写問題（Photographs）**
　1枚の写真に対して英文が4つ読まれ、最も適切に写真を描写しているものを選ぶ問題。英文は問題冊子に印刷されていません。各問題の解答時間（問題間のポーズ）は約5秒です。

● **Part 2　応答問題（Question-Response）**
　最初に話し手が質問・発言し、それに対する3つの応答の中から最も適切なものを選ぶ問題。質問・発言と応答は問題冊子に印刷されていません。各問題の解答時間は約5秒です。

● **Part 3　会話問題（Conversations）**
　2人または3人の会話に関する設問に答える問題。各会話に設問が3つあり、それぞれ4つの選択肢から最も適切な答えを選びます。設問と選択肢は問題冊子に印刷されていますが、会話は印刷されていません。後半に図表を見ながら答える設問も出題されます。各設問の解答時間は約8秒ですが、図表問題のみ約12秒に設定されています。

● **Part 4　説明文問題（Talks）**
　1人の話し手による放送（説明文）を聞いて、その内容に関する設問に答える問題。各説明文の設問と選択肢の数などは Part 3 と同様です。後半に図表を見ながら答える設問も出題されます。各設問の解答時間は約8秒ですが、図表問題のみ約12秒に設定されています。

● **Part 5　短文穴埋め問題（Incomplete Sentences）**
　文中の空所に入る最も適切な語句を4つの選択肢から選ぶ問題。

● **Part 6　長文穴埋め問題（Text Completion）**
　記事、手紙、メモなどの文書中に設けられた空所に入る最も適切な語句・文を4つの選択肢から選ぶ問題。各文書に4つの設問があります。

● **Part 7　読解問題（Reading Comprehension）**
　手紙、Eメール、記事、広告などの文書を読み、その内容に関する設問に答える問題。4つの選択肢から答えを選びます。Single Passage とよばれる「1つの文書」に対する設問は2～4問で計10セット29問、Double Passage とよばれる「2つの文書」に対する設問は5問で計2セット10問、Triple Passage とよばれる「3つの文書」に対する設問は5問で計3セット15問が出題されます。

本書の構成と効果的な使い方

　本書は全 12 ユニットで構成されており、巻頭に Pre-test（50 問：約 35 分）、Teacher's Manual（教授用書）に Post-test（50 問：約 35 分）を収録しています。また、各ユニットの後半にはリスニング、リーディングすべてのパートの練習問題に取り組む MINI TOEIC L&R TEST（約 20 分）を配しており、スコア記録表を巻末（p. 144）に収めています。Pre-test は学習前の実力診断に、Post-test は学習効果の診断にご利用ください。

> **注意**
> Pre-test と Post-test の音声は、教師用 CD だけに収録されています。

ユニット構成
　各ユニットは次のような構成になっています。

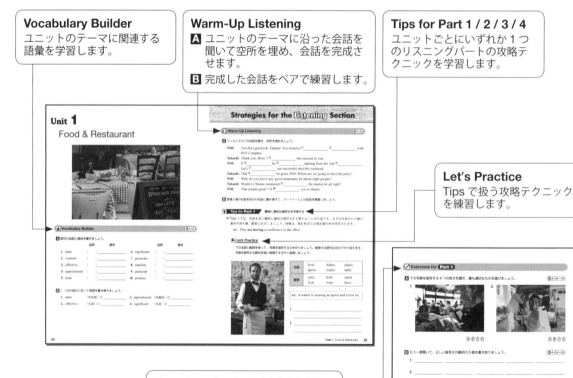

Strategies for the Reading Section

Warm-Up Reading
- **A** ユニットのテーマに沿った文章を読んで速読の練習をします。Part 7 のスコアを上げるポイントのひとつはスピードです。
- **B** 英文の内容に関する質問に答え、正確に内容が理解できているか確認します。

wpm の計算式：word 数÷所要時間（秒）× 60

Grammar Points
Part 5 と Part 6 に頻出する文法項目を簡潔に説明しています。

Tips for Part 5 / 6 / 7
ユニットごとにいずれか1つのリーディングパートの攻略テクニックを学習します。

Exercises for Part 5 / 6 / 7
Tips で扱うパートの実践問題です。学習した攻略テクニックを使って解き、本番でのスコアアップに繋げます。

MINI TOEIC L&R TEST

Listening Section（10問：約10分）＋ Reading Section（10問：約10分）
　各ユニットの学習内容の定着を図り、実際の *TOEIC*® Listening & Reading Test の問題形式に慣れるように工夫されています。巻末の表（p. 144）に自分の得点を記録しましょう。

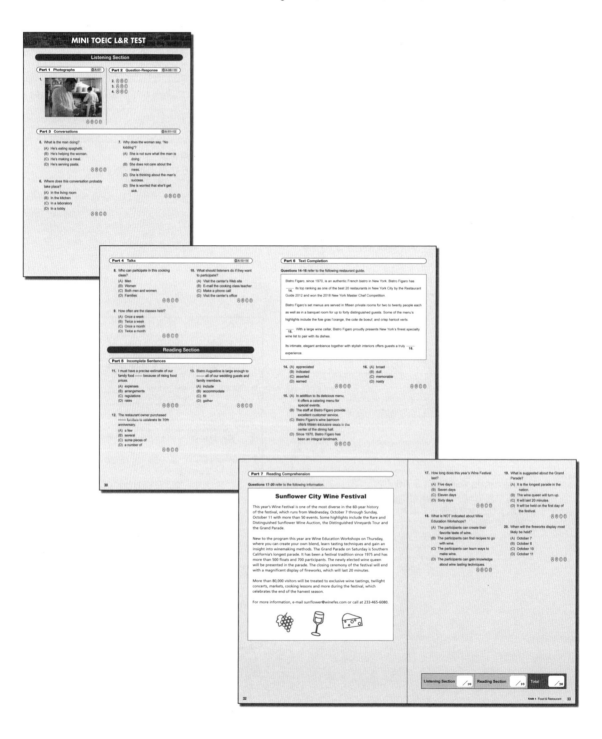

音声ファイルの利用方法

各ユニットの音声ファイル 🔊 にアクセスできます。

https://ngljapan.com/fastpasstoeic-re-audio/

① 上記 URL にアクセス、または QR コードをスマートフォンなどのリーダーでスキャン
② 表示されるファイル名をクリックして音声ファイルをダウンロード、または再生

無料のオンライン学習ツール Quizlet でボキャビル！

https://quizlet.com/NGL　Japan/folders/
fast-pass-for-the-toeic-lr-test/sets

上記 URL にパソコンでアクセス、または QR コードをスマートフォンなどのリーダーでスキャンすると、各ユニットの 👍 Vocabulary Builder A で取り上げている語句をクイズ形式で手軽に学習することができます。

Pre-test

（問題の音声はTeacher's CDに収録されています）

LISTENING TEST

● CD T-02〜04

In the Listening test, you will be asked to demonstrate how well you understand spoken English. The entire Listening test will last approximately 15 minutes. There are four parts, and directions are given for each part. You must mark your answers on the separate answer sheet. Do not write your answers in your test book.

PART 1

Directions: For each question in this part, you will hear four statements about a picture in your test book. When you hear the statements, you must select the one statement that best describes what you see in the picture. Then find the number of the question on your answer sheet and mark your answer. The statements will not be printed in your test book and will be spoken only one time.

Statement (C), "They're sitting at a table," is the best description of the picture, so you should select answer (C) and mark it on your answer sheet

Pre-test

1.

Ⓐ Ⓑ Ⓒ Ⓓ

2.

Ⓐ Ⓑ Ⓒ Ⓓ

PART 2

CD T-05〜13

Directions: You will hear a question or statement and three responses spoken in English. They will not be printed in your test book and will be spoken only one time. Select the best response to the question or statement and mark the letter (A), (B), or (C) on your answer sheet.

3. Ⓐ Ⓑ Ⓒ
4. Ⓐ Ⓑ Ⓒ
5. Ⓐ Ⓑ Ⓒ
6. Ⓐ Ⓑ Ⓒ
7. Ⓐ Ⓑ Ⓒ
8. Ⓐ Ⓑ Ⓒ
9. Ⓐ Ⓑ Ⓒ
10. Ⓐ Ⓑ Ⓒ

GO ON TO THE NEXT PAGE

PART 3

Directions: You will hear some conversations between two or more people. You will be asked to answer three questions about what the speakers say in each conversation. Select the best response to each question and mark the letter (A), (B), (C), or (D) on your answer sheet. The conversations will not be printed in your test book and will be spoken only one time.

11. What kind of company do the speakers probably work for?
    (A) Automobile manufacturing
    (B) Solar energy
    (C) Market research
    (D) Electric appliance
    Ⓐ Ⓑ Ⓒ Ⓓ

12. What does the woman say about the sales figures?
    (A) She says they went down.
    (B) She says they were doubled.
    (C) She says they were increased.
    (D) She says she didn't expect this much growth.
    Ⓐ Ⓑ Ⓒ Ⓓ

13. Who most likely is Jonathan?
    (A) Their client
    (B) Their rival
    (C) Their boss
    (D) Their co-worker
    Ⓐ Ⓑ Ⓒ Ⓓ

14. Where most likely are the speakers?
    (A) In a meeting room
    (B) On a tour bus
    (C) In Montreal
    (D) In Boston
    Ⓐ Ⓑ Ⓒ Ⓓ

15. What does the man say about Dr. Smith?
    (A) He has worked with Dr. Smith in the past.
    (B) He met Dr. Smith once at the research center.
    (C) He met Dr. Smith some time ago.
    (D) He has never met Dr. Smith.
    Ⓐ Ⓑ Ⓒ Ⓓ

16. What will probably happen next?
    (A) The woman will inquire about Dr. Smith.
    (B) The woman will attend a meeting.
    (C) The man will see Dr. Smith.
    (D) The man will leave the premises.
    Ⓐ Ⓑ Ⓒ Ⓓ

ADMISSION FEE	
Adults	$25
Seniors	$18 (65 and over with ID)
Children	$7 (Free 16 and under)

17. Where does this conversation probably take place?
    (A) In a restaurant
    (B) At a station
    (C) At a museum
    (D) In a movie theater

18. What does the man mean when he says, "No kidding"?
    (A) He doesn't want to make any comments.
    (B) He doesn't like the way the woman does things.
    (C) He doesn't like the modern art.
    (D) He doesn't want to walk for a long time.

19. Look at the graphic. How much is each speaker going to pay for the admission fee?
    (A) $7
    (B) $18
    (C) $25
    (D) $65

GO ON TO THE NEXT PAGE

PART 4

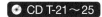

Directions: You will hear some talks given by a single speaker. You will be asked to answer three questions about what the speaker says in each talk. Select the best response to each question and mark the letter (A), (B), (C), or (D) on your answer sheet. The talks will not be printed in your test book and will be spoken only one time.

20. What is the talk mainly about?
    (A) A fruit drink
    (B) A new fitness center
    (C) A TV commercial
    (D) An upgraded product

21. Who most likely is the speaker?
    (A) A manager
    (B) A model
    (C) A designer
    (D) A fitness specialist

22. What does the speaker say he expects from his audience?
    (A) A round of applause
    (B) A way to cut costs
    (C) Good sales promotion
    (D) More individuality

23. What line of business does the speaker work in?
    (A) Finance
    (B) Food service
    (C) Tourism
    (D) Personnel placement

24. What is being announced?
    (A) The scheduled closure of some restaurants
    (B) The scheduled closure of all restaurants
    (C) The opening of a new branch
    (D) The takeover of another firm

25. What does the speaker say about the Lake Avenue establishment?
    (A) It will probably be the first to open.
    (B) It will probably be the first to close.
    (C) It will probably be renamed.
    (D) It will probably move to another location.

This is the end of the Listening test.
Turn to Part 5 in your test book.

READING TEST

In the Reading test, you will read a variety of texts and answer several different types of reading comprehension questions. The entire Reading test will last 20 minutes. There are three parts, and directions are given for each part. You are encouraged to answer as many questions as possible within the time allowed.

You must mark your answers on the separate answer sheet. Do not write your answers in your test book.

PART 5

Directions: A word or phrase is missing in each of the sentences below. Four answer choices are given below each sentence. Select the best answer to complete the sentence. Then mark the letter (A), (B), (C), or (D) on your answer sheet.

26. The ancient Egypt exhibition will be on ------- at the City Museum from April 23 to June 2.
    (A) installation
    (B) appearance
    (C) display
    (D) impression

27. You will be inviting the anger of the supervisor if you don't ------- your proposal by the deadline.
    (A) specify
    (B) appoint
    (C) submit
    (D) state

28. The head of the budget committee pointed out that the figures in our expense report were far from -------.
    (A) precise
    (B) precisely
    (C) precision
    (D) precisionism

29. The camera in my friend's mobile phone compares ------- to my digital camera.
    (A) favored
    (B) favorite
    (C) favorably
    (D) favorable

GO ON TO THE NEXT PAGE

30. Mike Mead, who works upstairs, ------- the raw materials used in manufacturing our products since we went into business.
(A) is handling
(B) handled
(C) had handled
(D) has been handling

31. This sunblock is not suitable ------- children under the age of three and those with sensitive skin.
(A) in
(B) with
(C) of
(D) for

32. It's best to avoid conflict, ------- I'd call that client and apologize if I were you.
(A) because
(B) so
(C) until
(D) since

33. Our company will hire twenty engineers ------- were laid off due to massive downsizing at the firm where they used to work.
(A) who
(B) whom
(C) which
(D) whose

34. The Gadget Store is by far the ------- of the two retail outlets owned and operated by Parker Electronics.
(A) good
(B) well
(C) better
(D) best

35. ------- of our orthopedic mattresses is tested and carefully inspected before being shipped.
(A) Some
(B) All
(C) Each
(D) Every

PART 6

Directions: Read the texts that follow. A word, phrase, or sentence is missing in parts of each text. Four answer choices for each question are given below the text. Select the best answer to complete the text. Then mark the letter (A), (B), (C), or (D) on your answer sheet.

Questions 36-39 refer to the following notice.

Recreation Center Closing due to Power Outage

From: Construction Project Manager

Please note that there will be a scheduled power outage in the Athletics Complex during the weekend of March 16 to 18 ------- install a new electric system in the New Steve Axer
36.
Sports and Fitness Center. Electric power will be cut off from 6:30 P.M. until 8:30 P.M. during these days. All athletics ------- except Cousens Gym will be impacted. These include
37.
Oleson Center, Lunder Fitness Center, and Chase Gym. Outdoor tennis courts will be closing earlier than usual, at 5:00 P.M. The telephone system ------- but computer services
38.
will not be available during the blackout.

-------. If you have any questions, please contact the Construction Project Manager at 617-
39.
627-5015.

Thank you for your cooperation.

36. (A) in order to
    (B) because of
    (C) so that
    (D) with regard to

37. (A) manufacturers
    (B) foundations
    (C) infrastructures
    (D) facilities

38. (A) function
    (B) will function
    (C) is functioned
    (D) to function

39. (A) Access to these buildings will be restricted during the power outage.
    (B) Once installed, it should increase the reliability of the power supply.
    (C) We apologize for the inconvenience caused by this unavoidable closure.
    (D) Departments which utilize electrical equipment are advised to plan for natural disasters.

GO ON TO THE NEXT PAGE

PART 7

Directions: In this part you will read a selection of texts, such as magazine and newspaper articles, e-mails, and instant messages. Each text or set of texts is followed by several questions. Select the best answer for each question and mark the letter (A), (B), (C), or (D) on your answer sheet.

Questions 40-41 refer to the following information.

South Lake Tahoe Nevada
Mackenzie HOTEL
At the Fun End of the Lake
800-511-1777

South Lake Tahoe is a wonderland for your favorite outdoor activities. It's a land of never-ending things to do. In winter, you can enjoy skiing and snowmobile tours at world-famous Heavenly Valley. In spring, the melting winter snow renews the glacial lake. The lifestyle changes to riding, cycling, and watching the wonders of the world. Summer comes early and stays late. You can go boating, swimming, golfing and fishing — all the enjoyment of nature. In fall, it's time for trail rides, fishing, and hunting in the crisp, clean air. South Lake Tahoe is a wonderful place to bring the family any time of year.

Deluxe Accommodations:

- 240 guest rooms
- Complimentary beverages
- Meeting and banquet facilities for 10 to 300 people
- Swimming pool and Jacuzzi
- Lilies Restaurant and Lounge
- Free guest parking
- Free local phone service

40. In which seasons is fishing recommended?
(A) Spring and summer
(B) Fall and winter
(C) Summer and fall
(D) Winter and spring

Ⓐ Ⓑ Ⓒ Ⓓ

41. Which service is NOT offered for free?
(A) Drinks
(B) Parking garage
(C) Breakfast
(D) Local phone calls

Ⓐ Ⓑ Ⓒ Ⓓ

Questions 42-45 refer to the following advertisement.

Free Coffee Machine for Your Office

Buy our coffee and get a free Italian Marion Coffee machine for your workplace. —[1]—. All you need to do is to purchase a minimum of 1kg of coffee beans per week. 1kg makes approximately 110 cups of coffee. Alternatively, if you don't think you will use that amount of coffee beans, you can rent the coffee machine for $22.00 per week.

Your coffee will be delivered to you at the start of each week. —[2]—. At less than 30 cents per cup, it makes quality coffee more affordable than from a coffee shop or a coffee vending machine.

—[3]—. Our coffee beans are freshly roasted right before they are delivered to you so they produce a satisfying drinking experience every time. Impress your clients and treat your staff to gourmet coffee every day. —[4]—.

This offer is available everywhere in Canada. For full details, contact sales@marioncoffee.com.

42. What type of business does Marion Coffee do?
    (A) It rents coffee vending machines.
    (B) It sells coffee machines.
    (C) It deals in coffee beans.
    (D) It operates a coffee shop.

43. Who would most likely be attracted by the advertisement?
    (A) Staff in a company who likes coffee
    (B) An employer who wants a coffee machine
    (C) A coffee machine supplier
    (D) Customers at a coffee shop

44. What is indicated about the service of Marion Coffee?
    (A) It can rent a coffee machine for $22 per month.
    (B) It offers a free coffee machine to the customers purchasing a certain amount of coffee beans.
    (C) The staff makes coffee at the customers' office for their clients.
    (D) Its product is delivered everywhere in Italy.

45. In which of the positions marked [1], [2], [3], and [4] does the following sentence best belong?

    "We will deliver and install our coffee machine without charge."
    (A) [1]
    (B) [2]
    (C) [3]
    (D) [4]

GO ON TO THE NEXT PAGE

Questions 46-50 refer to the following advertisement and e-mail.

ACCOUNTANT WANTED

Wednesday, January 15

E-mail: Click here to contact advertiser
Mobile phone: 080-500-6679
Message: Need accountant that can multitask. Must have good understanding of P & L and balance sheet reconciliation – ERP software data entry. BS in Accounting from accredited Taiwanese university required. Applicants must be able to read, write and speak English fluently. Send résumé and two recommendations by the end of this month to Kate Ryu.

From: Jane Watanabe
To: Kate Ryu
Subject: Accountant Position
Sent: Tue. 1/21 9:13 P.M.

Dear Ms. Ryu,

   This is in response to your advertisement in *JobSeeking* last week regarding a job vacancy for the position of accountant. I am greatly interested in the position and would like to apply for the job. I am submitting my résumé for your perusal and will submit my recommendations at your request.
   I am an accountancy graduate from a school known for its excellence in the field. I worked for five years as an accountant for Central Taiwan Bank but I had to leave the job to relocate with my family. I believe that I have the qualities you are looking for in an accountant. I hope to personally discuss with you in an interview how I can be an asset to your company.
   Thank you and I hope for your positive response.

Sincerely,
Jane Watanabe

46. Which of the following is NOT mentioned as a requirement for the position?
(A) P & L and balance sheet reconciliation
(B) Fluency in English
(C) ERP software data entry
(D) An MS in Accounting

Ⓐ Ⓑ Ⓒ Ⓓ

47. By what date should applicants respond to Kate Ryu?
(A) January 15
(B) January 21
(C) January 31
(D) February 28

Ⓐ Ⓑ Ⓒ Ⓓ

48. What is the purpose of this e-mail?
(A) To discuss a topic
(B) To apply for a position
(C) To submit an assignment
(D) To respond to a question

Ⓐ Ⓑ Ⓒ Ⓓ

49. Why did Ms. Watanabe leave her former position?
(A) For family relocation
(B) For financial reasons
(C) For commuting problems
(D) For physical reasons

Ⓐ Ⓑ Ⓒ Ⓓ

50. In the e-mail, the word "vacancy" in paragraph 1, line 2 is closest in meaning to
(A) admission
(B) cancellation
(C) information
(D) opening

Ⓐ Ⓑ Ⓒ Ⓓ

Stop! This is the end of the test. If you finish before time is called, you may go back to Parts 5, 6, and 7 and check your work.

Unit 1
Food & Restaurant

👍 Vocabulary Builder 🔊 A-02

A 語句の品詞と意味を書きましょう。

	品詞	意味		品詞	意味
1. taste	( ) _____		6. significant	( ) _____
2. contract	( ) _____		7. groceries	( ) _____
3. effective	( ) _____		8. nutrient	( ) _____
4. appointment	( ) _____		9. pesticide	( ) _____
5. treat	( ) _____		10. produce	( ) _____

B [ ]内の指示に従って単語を書き換えましょう。

1. taste   [形容詞] ⇨ _____   3. appointment [同義語] ⇨ _____
2. effective   [名詞]   ⇨ _____   4. significant [名詞]   ⇨ _____

Strategies for the Listening Section

🎧 Warm-Up Listening　　　　　　　　　　　　　　　　　　　　　　　A-03

A ウィルとタカシの会話を聞き、空所を埋めましょう。

Will: You did a good job, Takashi. You closed a ①_____ ②_____ with RST Company.
Takashi: Thank you, Boss. I ③_____ this success to you.
Will: It ④_____ be ⑤_____ starting from the 2nd ⑥_____. Let's ⑦_____ our successful deal this weekend.
Takashi: That ⑧_____ be great, Will! Where are we going to have the party?
Will: Well, do you know any good restaurants for about eight people?
Takashi: Would a Chinese restaurant ⑨_____ the station be all right?
Will: That sounds great. I'll ⑩_____ you to dinner.

B 登場人物の名前を自分の名前に置き換えて、パートナーと上の会話を練習しましょう。

💡 *Tips for* Part 1　　瞬時に適切な描写文を予想する

✔ Part 1 では、写真を見て瞬時に適切な描写文を予想することが大切です。まずは写真中の人物の動作や持ち物、服装に注目しましょう。時制は、現在形または現在進行形が多用されます。

　　ex. They **are having** a conference in the office.

🎤 Let's Practice

下の名詞と動詞を使って、写真を描写する文を作りましょう。修飾する語句は自分で付け加えます。写真を描写する語句を短い時間ですばやく推測しましょう。

名詞	food	dishes	plates
	apron	waiter	table
動詞	carry	hold	stand
	look	wear	have

ex. A waiter is wearing an apron and a bow tie.

1. _____

2. _____

Exercises for Part 1

A 下の写真を描写する４つの英文を聞き、最も適切なものを選びましょう。　　A-04〜05

1.2.

Ⓐ Ⓑ Ⓒ Ⓓ　　　　　　　　　　　　　　　　Ⓐ Ⓑ Ⓒ Ⓓ

B もう一度聞いて、正しい描写文の最初の５語を書き取りましょう。　　A-04〜05

1. _____ _____ _____ _____ _____

2. _____ _____ _____ _____ _____

Strategies for the Reading Section

Warm-Up Reading   A-06

A 英文を流れに沿って理解し、スピードを意識して速読しましょう。

Grocery stores sell fruits and vegetables from many different places. Have you ever wondered which to choose and why? Here are some good reasons to buy locally produced food. Firstly, locally produced food is fresher and tastier than the food produced in other regions or countries. Food grown in your community was picked within the past day or two. It is loaded with flavor and has not lost nutrients due to shipping. In addition, locally produced food is safer than the food produced in other countries. You have the power to ensure that the food you buy is free of pesticides, hormones, and antibiotics. Moreover, eating locally produced food has a positive effect on the environment. Transportation of food grown locally does not consume much fossil fuel, which means less pollution. So, seek out locally produced food at your supermarket.

(140 words) time [ ] wpm [ ]

B 上の英文の内容に関する質問に英語で答えましょう。

1. What is the topic of the passage?
   _____

2. Why is the locally produced food fresher and tastier than the food delivered from other regions or countries?
   _____

3. How does eating locally produced food affect the environment?
   _____

Grammar Points 名詞

可算名詞と不可算名詞：可算名詞（数えられる名詞）には単数形と複数形があり、単数の場合には冠詞のa/anやtheが前につく。不可算名詞（数えられない名詞）に複数形はなく、冠詞のa/anはつかない。不可算名詞の数え方は名詞によって異なるので、チェックしよう！

ex. There are an **apple** and five **oranges** in the **refrigerator**.（可算名詞）
There is some **cheese** and **milk** in the **refrigerator**.（不可算名詞）

また、factやideaなどは抽象的なものでも可算名詞で、bread、cheese、soapなど可算名詞と思われるようなものでも不可算名詞のものが多くある。

Unit 1 Food & Restaurant   27

Grammar Quiz （　）内の正しい語を○で囲みましょう。

1. The grocery store nearby the station sells many kinds of (fish / fishes).
2. Replacing all the (equipment / equipments) in our restaurant costs a lot of money.
3. My mother asked me to buy a (loaf / lump) of bread and a jar of marmalade.

Tips for Part 5　　問題のタイプを見分ける

✔ Part 5 と Part 6 では、語彙の問題と文法の問題が出されます。どちらに関する問題なのかを判断し、語彙の問題では文全体の意味を理解してから適切な語句を選びましょう。

ex. The guide explained how the old castle was ------- by the state government last year.
　　(A) invented　　(B) recalled　　(C) restored　　(D) surrounded

選択肢がすべて過去分詞 → 語彙の問題 → 文の意味を取る

ヒント「ガイドは、古い城がどのように州政府によって昨年 ------- されたかを説明しました」

Exercises for Part 5

文を完成させるのに、最も適切なものを選びましょう。

1. My coworker asked where he could find the most ------- restaurant near his apartment.
   (A) identical　　(B) economic　　(C) detailed　　(D) affordable

2. Since last year, my family has started a dinner ------- of taking turns telling the best and worst parts of our day.
   (A) obligation　　(B) ritual　　(C) policy　　(D) presentation

3. My mother would be ------- if her hotel room were not gorgeous and clean.
   (A) satisfied　　(B) disappointed　　(C) pleased　　(D) exhausted

4. The hotel concierge ------- making a reservation at the best Italian restaurant in town.
   (A) supervised　　(B) commented　　(C) recommended　　(D) provided

5. My mother asked me to buy ------- lettuce at the supermarket.
   (A) a head of　　(B) a bunch of　　(C) a stick of　　(D) a loaf of

MINI TOEIC L&R TEST

Listening Section

Part 1 Photographs A-07

1.

Ⓐ Ⓑ Ⓒ Ⓓ

Part 2 Question-Response A-08~10

2. Ⓐ Ⓑ Ⓒ
3. Ⓐ Ⓑ Ⓒ
4. Ⓐ Ⓑ Ⓒ

Part 3 Conversations A-11~12

5. What is the man doing?
   (A) He's eating spaghetti.
   (B) He's helping the woman.
   (C) He's making a meal.
   (D) He's serving pasta.
   Ⓐ Ⓑ Ⓒ Ⓓ

6. Where does this conversation probably take place?
   (A) In the living room
   (B) In the kitchen
   (C) In a laboratory
   (D) In a lobby
   Ⓐ Ⓑ Ⓒ Ⓓ

7. Why does the woman say, "No kidding"?
   (A) She is not sure what the man is doing.
   (B) She does not care about the mess.
   (C) She is thinking about the man's success.
   (D) She is worried that she'll get sick.
   Ⓐ Ⓑ Ⓒ Ⓓ

Part 4 Talks

8. Who can participate in this cooking class?
   (A) Men
   (B) Women
   (C) Both men and women
   (D) Families

9. How often are the classes held?
   (A) Once a week
   (B) Twice a week
   (C) Once a month
   (D) Twice a month

10. What should listeners do if they want to participate?
    (A) Visit the center's Web site
    (B) E-mail the cooking class teacher
    (C) Make a phone call
    (D) Visit the center's office

Reading Section

Part 5 Incomplete Sentences

11. I must have a precise estimate of our family food ------- because of rising food prices.
    (A) expenses
    (B) arrangements
    (C) regulations
    (D) rates

12. The restaurant owner purchased ------- furniture to celebrate its 30th anniversary.
    (A) a few
    (B) several
    (C) some pieces of
    (D) a number of

13. Bistro Augustine is large enough to ------- all of our wedding guests and family members.
    (A) include
    (B) accommodate
    (C) fill
    (D) gather

Part 6 Text Completion

Questions 14-16 refer to the following restaurant guide.

Bistro Figaro, since 1970, is an authentic French bistro in New York. Bistro Figaro has ------- (14.) its top ranking as one of the best 20 restaurants in New York City by the Restaurant Guide 2012 and won the 2018 New York Master Chef Competition.

Bistro Figaro's set menus are served in fifteen private rooms for two to twenty people each as well as in a banquet room for up to forty distinguished guests. Some of the menu's highlights include the foie gras l'orange, the cote de boeuf, and crisp haricot verts.

------- (15.) With a large wine cellar, Bistro Figaro proudly presents New York's finest specialty wine list to pair with its dishes.

Its intimate, elegant ambience together with stylish interiors offers guests a truly ------- (16.) experience.

14. (A) appreciated
    (B) indicated
    (C) asserted
    (D) earned

15. (A) In addition to its delicious menu, it offers a catering menu for special events.
    (B) The staff at Bistro Figaro provide excellent customer service.
    (C) Bistro Figaro's wine barroom offers fifteen exclusive seats in the center of the dining hall.
    (D) Since 1970, Bistro Figaro has been an integral landmark.

16. (A) broad
    (B) dull
    (C) memorable
    (D) nasty

Part 7   Reading Comprehension

Questions 17-20 refer to the following information.

Sunflower City Wine Festival

This year's Wine Festival is one of the most diverse in the 60-year history of the festival, which runs from Wednesday, October 7 through Sunday, October 11 with more than 50 events. Some highlights include the Rare and Distinguished Sunflower Wine Auction, the Distinguished Vineyards Tour and the Grand Parade.

New to the program this year are Wine Education Workshops on Thursday, where you can create your own blend, learn tasting techniques and gain an insight into winemaking methods. The Grand Parade on Saturday is Southern California's longest parade. It has been a festival tradition since 1975 and has more than 500 floats and 700 participants. The newly elected wine queen will be presented in the parade. The closing ceremony of the festival will end with a magnificent display of fireworks, which will last 20 minutes.

More than 80,000 visitors will be treated to exclusive wine tastings, twilight concerts, markets, cooking lessons and more during the festival, which celebrates the end of the harvest season.

For more information, e-mail sunflower@winefes.com or call at 233-465-6080.

17. How long does this year's Wine Festival last?
    (A) Five days
    (B) Seven days
    (C) Eleven days
    (D) Sixty days

18. What is NOT indicated about Wine Education Workshops?
    (A) The participants can create their favorite taste of wine.
    (B) The participants can find recipes to go with wine.
    (C) The participants can learn ways to make wine.
    (D) The participants can gain knowledge about wine tasting techniques.

19. What is suggested about the Grand Parade?
    (A) It is the longest parade in the nation.
    (B) The wine queen will turn up.
    (C) It will last 20 minutes.
    (D) It will be held on the first day of the festival.

20. When will the fireworks display most likely be held?
    (A) October 7
    (B) October 8
    (C) October 10
    (D) October 11

Listening Section /10 | Reading Section /10 | Total /20

Unit 2
Entertainment

👍 Vocabulary Builder　　　　　　　　　　　　🔊 A-15

A 語句の品詞と意味を書きましょう。

	品詞　意味		品詞　意味
1. audience	(　)　_____	6. choreography	(　)　_____
2. contribute	(　)　_____	7. matinee	(　)　_____
3. feature	(　)　_____	8. landmark	(　)　_____
4. admission fee	(　)　_____	9. impress	(　)　_____
5. box office	(　)　_____	10. award	(　)　_____

B [ ] 内の指示に従って単語を書き換えましょう。

1. audience　　[同義語] ⇨ _____　　3. matinee　　[反意語] ⇨ _____
2. contribute　[名詞] ⇨ _____　　4. impress　　[名詞] ⇨ _____

34

Strategies for the Listening Section

🎧 Warm-Up Listening 🔊 A-16

A アンとメグの会話を聞き、空所を埋めましょう。

Anne: Meg, I'd like to see a musical in the ①_____ next Saturday. Do you have any suggestions for ②_____?

Meg: Well, I hear some fabulous musicals are on the ③_____.

Anne: Oh, any musical will ④_____.

Meg: OK, then, how about seeing *The Chase*, which ⑤_____ a smart ⑥_____? They say its ⑦_____ is amazing.

Anne: Sounds interesting. I'd like to see the matinee. Is that ⑧_____ for you?

Meg: Sure. Let's meet at the ⑨_____ ⑩_____ at one o'clock.

B 登場人物の名前を自分の名前に置き換えて、パートナーと上の会話を練習しましょう。

💡 Tips for Part 2 質問文の最初の語をとらえる

✔ Part 2 は質問文・発話文および応答文が問題用紙に書かれていないため、集中力を要するパートです。音声による情報だけで質問・発話に対する正しい応答を選びます。質問文は最初の疑問詞や助動詞などをキャッチできれば、正答を選ぶのが容易になります。

🎧 Let's Practice

各質問に合う応答を1つ選びましょう。質問の意味をよく考えて判断しましょう。

1. When are you leaving for New York?
   (A) Only he knew.
   (B) Yes, he's leaving safely.
   (C) I haven't decided yet.
   Ⓐ Ⓑ Ⓒ

2. What does he look like?
   (A) I lived there for two months.
   (B) Just like his mother.
   (C) He likes oranges.
   Ⓐ Ⓑ Ⓒ

3. Where are they going to have the conference?
   (A) Sure, they are.
   (B) In Room 5.
   (C) We're going to lunch.
   Ⓐ Ⓑ Ⓒ

4. Why is her plane delayed?
   (A) Because of the communication gap.
   (B) Her plane is arriving late.
   (C) We haven't got any information yet.
   Ⓐ Ⓑ Ⓒ

Exercises for Part 2

A 質問に対する3つの応答を聞き、最も適切なものを選びましょう。　A-17〜19

1. Ⓐ Ⓑ Ⓒ
2. Ⓐ Ⓑ Ⓒ
3. Ⓐ Ⓑ Ⓒ

B もう一度聞いて、質問の最初の4語を書き取りましょう。　A-17〜19

1. _____ _____ _____ _____ going to be held?

2. _____ _____ _____ _____ to pay for the tickets?

3. _____ _____ _____ _____ performance start?

Strategies for the Reading Section

📖 Warm-Up Reading　　　　　　　　　　　　　　🔊 A-20

A 英文を流れに沿って理解し、スピードを意識して速読しましょう。

　　Broadway shows are one of the most popular tourist attractions in New York City. There are forty professional theaters in the Theater District. While many visitors in New York consider seeing a blockbuster Broadway show an essential experience, it can be hard to choose one from so many different shows. The longest-running musical in Broadway history is *The Phantom of the Opera* which opened on Broadway in 1988. It is the most financially successful Broadway show and won the 1988 Tony Award for Best Musical. Several long-running shows, such as *Cats, Chicago,* and *The Lion King*, are still playing today. When travelers are planning to see a Broadway show, they should start doing their research as soon as they book their stay in New York.

(125 words)　time [　　]　wpm [　　]

B 上の英文の内容に関する質問に英語で答えましょう。

1. How many professional theaters are there in the Theater District?
　_____

2. Why is it difficult to decide which show to see?
　_____

3. What do *Cats, Chicago,* and *The Lion King* have in common?
　_____

Grammar Points ｜ 代名詞

代名詞には話し手や相手、それ以外の人や物を表す人称代名詞、this や that など特定の人や物、語句などを指し示す指示代名詞、不特定の人や物、数量などを表す不定代名詞などがある。代名詞の it は主語として時間や天候、距離などを表したり、形式主語となることができる。

ex. How long will **it** take to get to the concert hall?（時間を表す主語）
　　It is certain that John will play the lead in the new musical.（that 以下を表す形式主語）
　　Mary bought an expensive camera, but I bought a cheap **one**.（不特定の物を指す）

one、all、both、either、neither などの不定代名詞に of がついたときは、これらの代名詞が単数・複数のどちらの扱いなのか、また、後に続く動詞が単数形か複数形かに注意しよう。

ex. **Both** of my sisters **are** going to the beach this weekend.

Grammar Quiz （ ）内の正しい語を○で囲みましょう。

1. I don't think that either of my sons (is / are) studying at home.
2. (All / Each) of the actors in that movie are capable and charming.
3. If you have any classical music CDs, I want to borrow (it / one).

Tips for Part 6　文の構造をしっかり把握する・文選択問題

✔ 文全体の構造を把握することは、適切な答えを選ぶカギとなります。主語（部）、述語動詞、補語または目的語などをしっかり把握してから、空所に入る品詞を特定しましょう。

ex. The video rental store in the shopping mall will ------- some DVDs to me tomorrow.
(A) delivery　　(B) deliver　　(C) deliverer　　(D) deliverable

ヒント The video rental から shopping mall までが文の主部。

✔ Part 6 では、適切な文を選択する問題が出題されます。空所の前後の文の内容に特に注意し、適切な文を選びましょう。前後の文だけで判断するのが難しい場合は、全体の流れや構成を把握することがポイントになります。

Exercises for Part 6

文を完成させるのに、最も適切なものを選びましょう。

Star Dance Next, the junior company of Sydney's Star Dance Theater, was formed in 1990 by the theater's ------- (1.) and artistic director, William Brown. ------- (2.). The company now performs all over the world, offering both concerts and educational programs. *Summer Riot* is Star Dance Next's annual summer season program, and performances are highly ------- (3.). This year, the company will present *Enjoy Your Cat* by choreographer, Phillip Adams. It will include live singing by Melissa Mauboy, a member of Australia's indigenous tribe. For more information about Star Dance Theater, visit www.stardance.org.

1. (A) founding　　(B) founder　　(C) found　　(D) foundation　　Ⓐ Ⓑ Ⓒ Ⓓ

2. (A) He was brought up in London, where he started dancing at the age of five.
   (B) Dancers are required to train year-round in the disciplines of ballet and jazz.
   (C) The junior company has taught dancers aged three to eighteen years old classical ballet.
   (D) It became a fully professional dance company three years later.
   　　Ⓐ Ⓑ Ⓒ Ⓓ

3. (A) anticipating　　(B) anticipation　　(C) anticipated　　(D) anticipate　　Ⓐ Ⓑ Ⓒ Ⓓ

MINI TOEIC L&R TEST

Listening Section

Part 1 Photographs ◉ A-21

1.

Ⓐ Ⓑ Ⓒ Ⓓ

Part 2 Question-Response ◉ A-22~24

2. Ⓐ Ⓑ Ⓒ
3. Ⓐ Ⓑ Ⓒ
4. Ⓐ Ⓑ Ⓒ

Part 3 Conversations ◉ A-25~26

5. Where is this conversation taking place?

   (A) In a restaurant
   (B) On a mountain
   (C) At a stadium
   (D) In a supermarket

   Ⓐ Ⓑ Ⓒ Ⓓ

6. What will the man most likely do next?

   (A) He will get a ticket.
   (B) He will play catch.
   (C) He will look for a seat.
   (D) He will get a snack.

   Ⓐ Ⓑ Ⓒ Ⓓ

7. What does the woman want?

   (A) A beverage
   (B) Potato chips
   (C) A sandwich
   (D) A hot dog and French fries

   Ⓐ Ⓑ Ⓒ Ⓓ

Part 4 Talks

🔊 A-27~28

8. What is this announcement mainly about?
   - (A) Hiking
   - (B) Intermission
   - (C) A meeting
   - (D) Nature conservation

   Ⓐ Ⓑ Ⓒ Ⓓ

9. When is the nature hike going to be held?
   - (A) This coming Sunday
   - (B) The day after tomorrow
   - (C) This coming Saturday
   - (D) Later today

   Ⓐ Ⓑ Ⓒ Ⓓ

10. What will be served at intermission?
    - (A) Nature hiking
    - (B) A bird's eye view
    - (C) Refreshments
    - (D) Some spaces

    Ⓐ Ⓑ Ⓒ Ⓓ

Reading Section

Part 5 Incomplete Sentences

11. ------- of my friends was nominated for the best picture award in the film festival.
    - (A) That
    - (B) Some
    - (C) Nobody
    - (D) One

    Ⓐ Ⓑ Ⓒ Ⓓ

12. My husband cut ------- while he was cooking my birthday dinner.
    - (A) himself
    - (B) him
    - (C) it
    - (D) itself

    Ⓐ Ⓑ Ⓒ Ⓓ

13. The chef demonstrated his ------- in cooking to the group at the cooking school.
    - (A) expert
    - (B) experts
    - (C) expertise
    - (D) expertizing

    Ⓐ Ⓑ Ⓒ Ⓓ

Part 6 Text Completion

Questions 14-16 refer to the following information.

The Sonoran Desert is a land of contradictions and many extremes. Widely considered to be the most visually ------- desert in the world, it contains a greater variety of plant life than
                                     14.
any other desert. Both botanists and zoologists consider it ------- of the richest regions on
                                                                       15.
earth. Plants from the bizarre boojum tree and saguaro cactus to the ponderosa pine are found in this region.

The Arizona-Sonora Desert Museum was founded in 1952 in order for visitors to gain knowledge and understanding about the Sonoran Desert region. On the museum grounds you will see more than 200 animal species and 1,200 kinds of plants on display — alive and in their natural desert setting. -------. Feel free to ask questions and interact with
                                                   16.
them. Their goal is to help you better understand this tough yet fragile environment.

14. (A) appeal
    (B) appeals
    (C) appealed
    (D) appealing

15. (A) some
    (B) all
    (C) one
    (D) each

16. (A) Trained museum volunteers give demonstrations every day.
    (B) Attractive picnic and camping facilities are available near the Museum.
    (C) The kids program is a great way for your preschoolers to learn about animals.
    (D) The museum provides a rewarding recreational opportunity for visitors of all ages.

Part 7   Reading Comprehension

Questions 17-20 refer to the following advertisement.

Silver Lake Music Festival

The Silver Lake Music Festival will be held at Midtown City Plaza on Saturday, July 25, and Sunday, July 26. The Silver Lake Music Festival Committee is now accepting artist applications for the festival. The festival features music in almost every genre imaginable — hip-hop, metal, rock, folk, electronic, and more. We are always seeking new and exciting musical performances. If you are interested in being a musical performer at Silver Lake, please complete an application online.

Deadlines & Important Dates

Friday, February 7:   Completed applications must be received by the Silver Lake Music Festival Committee no later than 5:00 P.M. Late applications will be accepted until February 25. Due to the volume of applicants, a $10 processing fee and a $10 late fee will be applied to applications.

Monday, April 6:   We will contact you if we are interested in pursuing a booking.

Friday, May 1:   Accepted performers are required to send signed contracts back to the festival committee no later than 5:00 P.M.

All music applications must be completed online.

17. For whom is the advertisement most likely intended?

(A) Festival committee staff
(B) Musical festival audiences
(C) Festival sponsors
(D) Music performers

Ⓐ Ⓑ Ⓒ Ⓓ

18. The word "features" in paragraph 1, line 4, is closest in meaning to

(A) qualifies
(B) highlights
(C) benefits
(D) coordinates

Ⓐ Ⓑ Ⓒ Ⓓ

19. How much should a person pay to apply for the event on February 11?

(A) Nothing
(B) 10 dollars
(C) 20 dollars
(D) 25 dollars

Ⓐ Ⓑ Ⓒ Ⓓ

20. When will an applicant receive a positive response from the festival committee?

(A) February 7
(B) April 6
(C) May 1
(D) July 25

Ⓐ Ⓑ Ⓒ Ⓓ

| Listening Section | /10 | Reading Section | /10 | Total | /20 |

Unit 3
Travel

🗣 Vocabulary Builder 🔊 A-29

A 語句の品詞と意味を書きましょう。

	品詞	意味		品詞	意味
1. flight	( )	_____	6. altitude	( )	_____
2. immigration	( )	_____	7. tax-free	( )	_____
3. fasten	( )	_____	8. delay	( )	_____
4. temperature	( )	_____	9. valid	( )	_____
5. luggage	( )	_____	10. equipment	( )	_____

B [ ]内の指示に従って単語を書き換えましょう。

1. immigration ［動詞］⇨ _____
2. luggage ［同義語］⇨ _____
3. valid ［名詞］⇨ _____
4. temperature の単位 ［摂氏］⇨ _____
   ［華氏］⇨ _____

Strategies for the Listening Section

🎧 Warm-Up Listening 🔊 A-30

A トオル、エミリー、店員（Clerk）の会話を聞き、空所を埋めましょう。

Toru: Excuse me, we'd like to buy two tickets to Madrid via Switzerland a week from ①_____. Are they ②_____?

Clerk: Just a second, please. ③_____ me check if there are any unoccupied seats left for you.

Toru: ④_____.

Emily: What shall we do if there are no tickets left, Toru? This is an ⑤_____.

Toru: Hopefully we can get ⑥_____ for some flight. Don't worry, Emily.

Clerk: Hmm, I can find only one seat unoccupied for the ⑦_____ A.M. flight.

Toru: Oh, no! We need them for both of ⑧_____.

Clerk: Well, wait, I ⑨_____ it. Both of you can get seats for the last flight, which ⑩_____ at 11:57 P.M. You want them for Madrid via Switzerland, right?

Toru: Exactly, ma'am.

B 登場人物の名前を自分の名前に置き換えて、パートナーと上の会話を練習しましょう。

💡 Tips for Part 3　3人の会話と話し手の意図を問う設問

✓ Part 3 では2人による会話だけではなく、3人による会話も出題されます。3人による会話は複雑になっているので前後関係をよく聞き取りましょう。また、ある表現が会話の中でどのような意味合いで使われているのか、話者の意図を問う問題も出題されます。会話の展開をしっかりと捉えて、文脈から意味を判断しましょう。

🎧 Let's Practice

"I got it." や "I can't believe it." などの表現は、前後関係で肯定的にも否定的にもとれる意味を持っています。I got it. の知っている意味を書いてみましょう。

_____　　_____　　_____

Exercises for Part 3

A 会話を聞いて、質問に対する正しい答えを選びましょう。　　　A-31

1. What is the man's occupation?
   - (A) A pilot
   - (B) A driver
   - (C) A flight attendant
   - (D) A customs official

   Ⓐ Ⓑ Ⓒ Ⓓ

2. Where do the women want to go after walking around?
   - (A) Central Park
   - (B) New York
   - (C) A Metro station
   - (D) A museum

   Ⓐ Ⓑ Ⓒ Ⓓ

3. What does the man mean when he says, "Let me tell you something"?
   - (A) He has a story to tell the women.
   - (B) He does not care about the women's destination.
   - (C) He has some advice for the women.
   - (D) He has some problems.

   Ⓐ Ⓑ Ⓒ Ⓓ

B もう一度聞いて、(　) に適語を入れましょう。　　　A-31

W1: Here's our (①　　　　　　　), Lucy. Come on!

M: Hi! Welcome to New York! Where (②　　　　　　　) I take you?

W1: Hi! We want to go to Central Park.

M: All right. (③　　　　　　　) to Central Park. Will you close the door?

W2: We are going to visit the Metropolitan (④　　　　　　　) (⑤　　　　　　　) walking around the park.

M: OK. Let me tell you something. It's really a (⑥　　　　　　　) park, you know. Too much walking is going to make you really tired.

W1: Yeah, that's true. We hope we don't get too (⑦　　　　　　　).

Strategies for the Reading Section

📖 Warm-Up Reading   🔊 A-32

A 英文を流れに沿って理解し、スピードを意識して速読しましょう。

Hawaii is famous for its marvelous natural landscapes. If you've only got three days, why not follow our suggestions? On the first day, begin your Hawaiian adventure in the traditional way by choosing a Hawaiian Lei greeting and a seamless airport transfer to your hotel. Enjoy a relaxing snorkel cruise or a Hawaiian dinner before watching a traditional Polynesian Luau show. The second day takes you on an exciting helicopter tour to see all of what the Big Island offers, such as rainforests, waterfalls, and ocean. On the last day, join a Kilauea Volcano adventure tour that features a walk over the lava flow that covered the village of Kalapana and the famous Kaimu black sand beach in the 1980's.

(120 words)   time [   ]   wpm [   ]

B 上の英文の内容に関する質問に英語で答えましょう。

1. For whom is the advertisement most likely intended?
   _____

2. What is suggested travelers do after enjoying a snorkel cruise or Hawaiian dinner?
   _____

3. What happened in the village of Kalapana in the 1980's?
   _____

Grammar Points | 助動詞

can の用法：「～できる」という能力や可能性を表す以外に、許可・依頼・申し出などを表す。
  ex. John **can** ride a horse.（能力）／ **Can** I call you tonight?（許可）

must の用法：「～しなければならない」という必要・義務を表す。must not は禁止を表す。
  ex. We **must** protect the environment.（義務）

would の用法：時制を一致させるときに will の過去として用いる。また、「～であろう」という推量、過去の不規則な習慣、丁寧な依頼などを表す場合にも用いる。
  ex. My brother and I **would** go fishing together.（習慣）
     Would you lend me your book?（丁寧な依頼）

※ must の「～に違いない」、cannot の「～のはずがない」という意味や、慣用表現の cannot help ~ing「～せざるを得ない」、may as well ＋ 動詞の原形「～するほうがよい」も覚えよう。

Unit 3 Travel

Grammar Quiz （　）内の正しい語句を○で囲みましょう。

1. You (cannot / would not) have seen Tim yesterday since he left for Rome two days ago.
2. (Could / Would) you mind carrying my suitcase to the hotel?
3. It (must / will) be true that many young people are addicted to fast food.

Tips for Part 7　スマホやパソコンでのインターネット会話に慣れよう

✔ スマホでの2人で行うメッセージチェーンや3人以上で行うオンラインディスカッションでは、人物の関係や場所を理解することが必要です。口語表現が用いられることにも注意しましょう。また、これらの文書では、メッセージやディスカッション中の1文を取り上げ、発信した人の意図を問う問題があり、それまでのやり取りの内容を正確に把握する必要があります。

Exercises for Part 7

次のメッセージチェーンを読み、質問に答えましょう。

Shiao-wen Kao　　　　　　　　　　　　　　　　　　　　8:05 P.M.
I would like to take my clients from Japan sightseeing this Saturday. Can you recommend some interesting places not too far from our office?

David Olson　　　　　　　　　　　　　　　　　　　　　8:07 P.M.
How about the Brownwood Bridge? You can enjoy walking across the bridge. Also, there are many shopping and dining places along the riverside.

Shiao-wen Kao　　　　　　　　　　　　　　　　　　　　8:08 P.M.
Sounds great! As I'm a newcomer, do you have any nice restaurants in mind?

David Olson　　　　　　　　　　　　　　　　　　　　　8:10 P.M.
Sure. Sam's Seafood House is a must-try, but if you want them to taste local food, Boulevard is the best.

Shiao-wen Kao　　　　　　　　　　　　　　　　　　　　8:11 P.M.
Local food is good. Will you give me more information about it?

David Olson　　　　　　　　　　　　　　　　　　　　　8:13 P.M.
I'd be pleased to help you.

---

1. Why does Ms. Kao contact Mr. Olson?
   (A) To visit the Brownwood Bridge.
   (B) To get an idea how to entertain her clients.
   (C) To find out the direction to a landmark.
   (D) To give information about her weekend plan.

   Ⓐ Ⓑ Ⓒ Ⓓ

2. At 8:13 P.M., what does Mr. Olson mean when he writes, "I'd be pleased to help you"?
   (A) He will go sightseeing with her clients.
   (B) He will give her more information about a seafood restaurant.
   (C) He will suggest which restaurant she should go to.
   (D) He will provide her with detailed information about Boulevard.

   Ⓐ Ⓑ Ⓒ Ⓓ

MINI TOEIC L&R TEST

Listening Section

Part 1 Photographs ◉ A-33

1.

   Ⓐ Ⓑ Ⓒ Ⓓ

Part 2 Question-Response ◉ A-34~36

2. Ⓐ Ⓑ Ⓒ
3. Ⓐ Ⓑ Ⓒ
4. Ⓐ Ⓑ Ⓒ

Part 3 Conversations ◉ A-37~38

5. Where are the speakers?
   (A) At a hotel
   (B) In the personnel department
   (C) At an airport
   (D) At a travel agency

   Ⓐ Ⓑ Ⓒ Ⓓ

6. Why can the woman choose a room?
   (A) Because it's off-season.
   (B) Because she is paying more.
   (C) Because the weather is terrible.
   (D) Because a mistake was made.

   Ⓐ Ⓑ Ⓒ Ⓓ

7. What kind of room would the woman like to have?
   (A) A top-story room
   (B) A slightly smaller room
   (C) A little larger room
   (D) A little cheaper room

   Ⓐ Ⓑ Ⓒ Ⓓ

Unit 3 Travel 49

Part 4 Talks

8. Where would this announcement be heard?
   - (A) At an airport
   - (B) In an airplane
   - (C) In a duty free shop
   - (D) At a subway station

9. How long will it take to New York?
   - (A) 10 hours and 30 minutes
   - (B) 12 hours and 13 minutes
   - (C) 12 hours and 30 minutes
   - (D) 20 hours and 13 minutes

10. According to the report, how is the weather in New York?
    - (A) Rainy
    - (B) Cloudy
    - (C) Windy and sunny
    - (D) Clear

Reading Section

Part 5 Incomplete Sentences

11. ------- you tell me how to buy a train ticket from a ticket machine?
    - (A) Must
    - (B) Could
    - (C) Have
    - (D) Should

12. Mary is absent from the monthly dinner party. She ------- have caught a cold.
    - (A) should
    - (B) will
    - (C) must
    - (D) can

13. My grandparents ------- often go out on long walks together when they were alive.
    - (A) should
    - (B) would
    - (C) must
    - (D) may

Part 6 Text Completion

Questions 14-16 refer to the following information.

Great Vacations in Florida

The Florida Keys, a chain of small islands, curves around the tip of Florida from the Atlantic Ocean to the Gulf of Mexico. You can enjoy the scenic sea on a daylong drive from Miami to Key West via the Overseas Highway. But it's much more fun to take time for leisurely island-hopping. Divers and snorkelers will want to get a view of underwater life and the coral reef at State Park, Key Largo. If you'd rather stay dry, go on a boat trip and ------- at tropical fish and turtles through the underwater windows. You can get a sense
14.
of the island's many attractions aboard the Conch Tour Train, ------- offers 90-minute
15.
narrated tours. -------. Museums and shops may also amuse you. But remember to take
16.
them in slowly — in relaxed Key West style.

14. (A) scold
    (B) stand
    (C) stare
    (D) stick

    Ⓐ Ⓑ Ⓒ Ⓓ

15. (A) that
    (B) which
    (C) where
    (D) whose

    Ⓐ Ⓑ Ⓒ Ⓓ

16. (A) You can rent a mask, snorkel and fins at the Marine Center.
    (B) The large glass bottom boats depart from here for tours.
    (C) There are plenty of great attractions and activities in these areas.
    (D) The ride includes three 10-minute stops where you can grab some cold drinks.

    Ⓐ Ⓑ Ⓒ Ⓓ

Part 7 Reading Comprehension

Questions 17-18 refer to the following memo.

Dear employees:

Annual Company Family Camping

We are proud to offer the annual Family Camping at White Mountains Park from July 24 to 26. Family Camping is a great way to spend uninterrupted time together while creating valuable memories. You can do many different activities each day, such as swimming, wildlife viewing, and canoeing. No previous experience is necessary to participate in these activities. The event includes camping and cooking equipment (except a sleeping bag), all meals, all camping fees, park fees, transportation, and professional guide service. Everybody is expected to participate in camp set-up and take-down. The company will provide snacks and drinks. We have to make a campsite reservation in advance. So if you are going, please call Steve Wilson at extension 6522 or e-mail him at swilson@ibengineering.com by July 15. We offer this camping event to employees and their families at a special price. To see the itinerary and the price, visit www.camp.ibengineering.com.

17. What will employees who are paticipating in the event probably do in advance?

    (A) Practice canoeing
    (B) Prepare a sleeping bag
    (C) Buy cooking equipment
    (D) Make a campsite reservation

18. What benefit will the employees participating in the event receive?

    (A) Free meals
    (B) Free professional guide service
    (C) Free transportation
    (D) Free snacks and beverages

Questions 19-20 refer to the following text message chain.

19. Why does Ms. Hamilton contact Mr. Wiley?

(A) She wants to book a flight.
(B) She wants to introduce her colleague to Mr. Wiley.
(C) She needs information on traffic.
(D) She needs to find a reasonable accommodation.

Ⓐ Ⓑ Ⓒ Ⓓ

20. At 2:16 P.M., what does Ms. Hamilton mean when she writes, "I'm counting on you"?

(A) She will seek an economy hotel.
(B) She expects to receive a positive reply from Mr. Wiley.
(C) She is anxiously awaiting Mr. Wiley's phone call.
(D) She will contact a hotel manager.

Ⓐ Ⓑ Ⓒ Ⓓ

Unit 4
Sports & Health

👍 Vocabulary Builder 🔊 A-41

A 語句の品詞と意味を書きましょう。

	品詞 意味		品詞 意味
1. amazing	( ) _____	6. moderator	( ) _____
2. junk food	( ) _____	7. obesity	( ) _____
3. fad	( ) _____	8. prescription	( ) _____
4. gigantic	( ) _____	9. avoid	( ) _____
5. stadium	( ) _____	10. outstanding	( ) _____

B [ ]内の指示に従って単語を書き換えましょう。

1. amazing   [動詞] ⇨ _____   3. obesity   [形容詞] ⇨ _____
2. gigantic   [同義語] ⇨ _____   4. prescription [動詞] ⇨ _____

Strategies for the Listening Section

🎧 Warm-Up Listening 　　　　　　　　　　　　　　　🔊 A-42

A アンとタカシの会話を聞き、空所を埋めましょう。

Anne: This is ①_____. I've never seen a ball game in a stadium.
Takashi: I'm glad you ②_____ ③_____, Anne.
Anne: I love to sing "Take Me Out to the Ball Game."
Takashi: Umm. OK, OK. This stadium is ④_____. It's about ⑤_____ square meters.
Anne: Let's take those seats over there. We can see ⑥_____ the pitcher throws the ball from the best ⑦_____.
Takashi: Sorry, but all the ⑧_____ are reserved, you know. Come this way.
Anne: Well, I'm ⑨_____ you. Hey, don't ⑩_____ me behind, Takashi!

B 登場人物の名前を自分の名前に置き換えて、パートナーと上の会話を練習しましょう。

💡 *Tips for* Part 4　　ざっくばらんな表現や音の脱落などに注意する

✔ かしこまった表現ではなく、ざっくばらんな表現 "well" "you know" や言いよどみ "umm"、音の脱落 "'cause" = because "'bout" = about などが使われることがあります。友達や同僚などの親しい間柄でのトークで使用されることが多いので、音に慣れておきましょう。

🎧 *Let's Practice*　　　　　　　　　　　　　　　🔊 A-43

次の音声を聞いて、最初の 4 語を書き取りましょう。

1. _____ _____ _____ _____ do tonight?

2. _____ _____ _____ _____ for dinner?

3. _____ _____ _____ _____ him since last week.

Exercises for Part 4

説明文を聞いて、質問に対する正しい答えを選びましょう。　　　A-44

1. What is the speaker mainly talking about?
   (A) The history of London
   (B) Information about entry
   (C) Qualifications for customers
   (D) How to fill out the entry form

   Ⓐ Ⓑ Ⓒ Ⓓ

2. How often is the event held?
   (A) Once a week
   (B) Once a month
   (C) Once a year
   (D) Once every two years

   Ⓐ Ⓑ Ⓒ Ⓓ

3. What does the speaker mean when she says, "But you've got to remember"?
   (A) To remind listeners of the importance of a deadline
   (B) To refer to exceptions for entry
   (C) To attract an interest in the merit of working out
   (D) To mention an upper age limit

   Ⓐ Ⓑ Ⓒ Ⓓ

Strategies for the Reading Section

Warm-Up Reading   A-45

A 英文を流れに沿って理解し、スピードを意識して速読しましょう。

Overweight and obesity are becoming serious health problems. They are the fifth leading risk for global deaths. According to the World Health Organization, approximately 1.9 billion adults were overweight and one third of this group was obese in 2016. Basically, overweight and obesity occur when people consume more calories than they burn. There are various causes for this, such as poor eating habits, lifestyle behaviors, and genetic factors. Overweight and obesity lead to serious health consequences. Overweight and obese people have a higher risk of getting heart disease. They also have breathing and sleeping problems. If you have a weight problem, you should change your eating habits, plan meals and make better food selections. Eat less fatty foods and avoid junk and fast foods. You also have to increase physical activity—get at least 30 minutes of moderate-intensity exercise regularly.

(140 words) | time [   ] | wpm [   ]

B 上の英文の内容に関する質問に英語で答えましょう。

1. What is the topic of the passage?
   _____

2. How many adults were overweight in 2016?
   _____

3. What kind of health problems do overweight and obese people have?
   _____

Grammar Points | 形容詞

形容詞には、名詞を修飾する**限定用法**と、文の補語として用いて主語や目的語を説明する**叙述用法**がある。限定用法、叙述用法のどちらか一方しかない形容詞もあるので注意しよう。

ex. He is an **outstanding** athlete. / I like to watch **professional** baseball games.
(限定用法)

Our school is **strong** in soccer. / He is **suitable** for the post of sales manager.
(叙述用法)

※限定用法のみの形容詞（例：main、rural、elder、名詞＋接尾辞 -en でできた形容詞）
　叙述用法のみの形容詞（例：worth、ready、接頭辞 a- の形容詞が多い）

Grammar Quiz (　) 内の正しい語を○で囲みましょう。

1. John could not join today's baseball game because of a (hard / serious) illness.
2. Olympic athletes are quite (capable / able) of withstanding various stresses.
3. Michel recalled his (alone / lonely) childhood while listening to a children's song.

Tips for Part 5　　語と語の意味の結びつきに注目する

✔ 空所の前後の名詞や動詞などが、空所に入る語句と強い意味の結びつきを持っている場合があるので、語と語の結びつきを理解することが、適切な答えを選ぶカギとなります。結びつきの強い単語は、一緒に覚えるようにしましょう。

下の文の空所に入る語で思いつくものを挙げましょう。

He reserved ------- for the annual conference.
　　　　　　　　a hotel,

A〔An〕------- number of people are estimated to take part in the sports event.
　　　　　　　　incredible,

このように語と語を関連付けて語彙を増やすことで、空所に入る語句をすばやく把握することができるようになります。

Exercises for Part 5

文を完成させるのに、最も適切なものを選びましょう。

1. Our team has to improve our fielding to ------- that team easily.
   (A) defeat　　(B) hit　　(C) conquer　　(D) win
   Ⓐ Ⓑ Ⓒ Ⓓ

2. You should ------- the seat of the exercise bike when using it at the gym.
   (A) regulate　　(B) modulate　　(C) arrange　　(D) adjust
   Ⓐ Ⓑ Ⓒ Ⓓ

3. Most patients in nursing homes will never ------- full health and never leave the nursing home.
   (A) return　　(B) regain　　(C) increase　　(D) retrieve
   Ⓐ Ⓑ Ⓒ Ⓓ

4. The doctor gave him a blood ------- and found a serious health problem.
   (A) investigation　　(B) experiment　　(C) test　　(D) survey
   Ⓐ Ⓑ Ⓒ Ⓓ

5. The company ------- a contract for constructing a new stadium.
   (A) signed　　(B) did　　(C) formed　　(D) tied
   Ⓐ Ⓑ Ⓒ Ⓓ

MINI TOEIC L&R TEST

Listening Section

Part 1 Photographs 🔊 A-46

1.

Ⓐ Ⓑ Ⓒ Ⓓ

Part 2 Question-Response 🔊 A-47~49

2. Ⓐ Ⓑ Ⓒ
3. Ⓐ Ⓑ Ⓒ
4. Ⓐ Ⓑ Ⓒ

Part 3 Conversations 🔊 A-50~51

5. Where most likely are the speakers?
   (A) In a restaurant
   (B) At a hotel
   (C) In a pharmacy
   (D) At a gym

   Ⓐ Ⓑ Ⓒ Ⓓ

6. How is the man going to pay?
   (A) By card
   (B) With insurance
   (C) By check
   (D) With cash

   Ⓐ Ⓑ Ⓒ Ⓓ

7. What is the man probably going to do next?
   (A) He's going to a doctor's office.
   (B) He's going to an insurance company.
   (C) He's going to see a nurse.
   (D) He's going to stay at the pharmacy.

   Ⓐ Ⓑ Ⓒ Ⓓ

Part 4 Talks 🔊 A-52~53

	10:00–10:50	11:00–11:50	12:00–12:50
Studio A	Barbell	Kickboxing	Jazz Dance
Studio B	Fit To the Core	Yoga	
Studio C		Cardio Fitness	Hip Hop
Studio D	Stretching		Basic Ballet

8. What is the speaker mainly talking about?
   (A) How to find a favorite fitness program
   (B) How to sign up for the fitness center
   (C) How to manage the diet program
   (D) How to join the yoga program
   Ⓐ Ⓑ Ⓒ Ⓓ

9. What program is the most appropriate if a person is keen on fitness?
   (A) Barbell
   (B) Hip Hop
   (C) Fit to the Core
   (D) Cardio Fitness
   Ⓐ Ⓑ Ⓒ Ⓓ

10. Look at the graphic. In which studio do they offer a very popular dancing program among young people?
    (A) Studio A
    (B) Studio B
    (C) Studio C
    (D) Studio D
    Ⓐ Ⓑ Ⓒ Ⓓ

Reading Section

Part 5 Incomplete Sentences

11. The golfer asked her caddy to ------- out the distance to the green.
    (A) calculate
    (B) measure
    (C) weigh
    (D) evaluate
    Ⓐ Ⓑ Ⓒ Ⓓ

12. College baseball coaches travel around the country and go to games to observe ------- athletes.
    (A) bright
    (B) speculative
    (C) prospective
    (D) perspective
    Ⓐ Ⓑ Ⓒ Ⓓ

13. Many farmers still use insecticides and chemical fertilizers to ------- production.
    (A) increase
    (B) advance
    (C) extend
    (D) progress
    Ⓐ Ⓑ Ⓒ Ⓓ

Part 6 Text Completion

Questions 14-16 refer to the following information.

Welcome to the Paradise Golf Club, the finest golf facility in North America. Our club is conveniently located just minutes from downtown Black Rock. We have 36 Championship golf holes divided into two great golf courses. The 18-hole courses provide a beautifully ------- oasis of green against the earth tones of the South Mountains. Besides our golf
14.
courses, we offer a state-of-the-art practice facility and a beautiful clubhouse.

Don't miss the Diamond Cup Golf Tournament held annually in June. -------.
15.

The Paradise Golf Club is membership owned by over 300 members. We provide professional services to our members and guests at very affordable -------.
16.

14. (A) retained
    (B) maintained
    (C) preserved
    (D) surrounded
    Ⓐ Ⓑ Ⓒ Ⓓ

15. (A) Our golf courses were designed by a world-renowned architect.
    (B) We offer the most impressive group of instructors in the state.
    (C) All the courses have numerous bunkers.
    (D) This event is open to the public and there is no admission fee.
    Ⓐ Ⓑ Ⓒ Ⓓ

16. (A) fines
    (B) costs
    (C) fares
    (D) rates
    Ⓐ Ⓑ Ⓒ Ⓓ

Part 7 Reading Comprehension

Questions 17-20 refer to the following advertisement.

Max Fitness Club

Home | Join Now | Locations | Classes | Contact Us

We'll help you get into shape.

Max Fitness Club is one of Australia's fastest growing fitness chains, providing our members with state-of-the-art equipment and facilities combined with first-class service, quality personal trainers, dietary supplements, and the latest in fitness apparel. For your convenience, we are open 24 hours a day, seven days a week.

Max Fitness Club offers a number of programs that will suit your fitness level and your busy schedule. We are always introducing new programs for you to participate in. Most classes are open to all members free of charge.

We will offer three new exercise classes starting July 1. On Mondays, enjoy an hour of Power Yoga and on Fridays, enjoy Belly Dancing. On Saturdays, join the Cardio Kickboxing class. All classes start at 10 A.M.

* **SUMMER Sales Event!** Until the end of July, Max Fitness Club is offering 15% off its membership fee for the year and 30% off if you join with a friend.
* **FREE 7-DAY Trial Pass** See why Max Fitness Club is just right for you. Simply complete the form and receive a FREE 7-DAY Trial Pass. **Click Here**

17. What is suggested about Max Fitness Club?
    (A) It is open around the clock.
    (B) It is located in major cities in North Australia.
    (C) It is looking for quality trainers.
    (D) All members can join every class for free.
    Ⓐ Ⓑ Ⓒ Ⓓ

18. The word "facilities" in paragraph 1, line 2 is closest in meaning to
    (A) means
    (B) skills
    (C) amenities
    (D) funds
    Ⓐ Ⓑ Ⓒ Ⓓ

19. How can a person get a 30% discount on membership?
    (A) By signing up at the club by the end of August
    (B) By entering the club with a friend
    (C) By taking part in a free 7-day trial
    (D) By joining new group lessons
    Ⓐ Ⓑ Ⓒ Ⓓ

20. Which new class will be held on Fridays in July?
    (A) Power Yoga
    (B) Belly Dancing
    (C) Cardio Kickboxing
    (D) Step Training
    Ⓐ Ⓑ Ⓒ Ⓓ

| Listening Section | /10 | Reading Section | /10 | Total | /20 |

Unit 5
Purchasing

Vocabulary Builder 🔊 A-54

A 語句の品詞と意味を書きましょう。

	品詞	意味		品詞	意味
1. package	( ) _____		6. fuel	( ) _____	
2. contain	( ) _____		7. warranty	( ) _____	
3. shelf	( ) _____		8. corporate	( ) _____	
4. insure	( ) _____		9. expiration	( ) _____	
5. fragile	( ) _____		10. overspend	( ) _____	

B [ ]内の指示に従って単語を書き換えましょう。

1. shelf　　　［複数形］⇨ _____　　3. warranty　　［動詞］⇨ _____
2. insure　　　［名詞］⇨ _____　　4. expiration　　［動詞］⇨ _____

Strategies for the Listening Section

🎧 Warm-Up Listening ◉ A-55

A 係員 (Clerk) とアンの会話を聞き、空所を埋めましょう。

Clerk: Hello, ma'am. May I help you?
Anne: ①_____ like to send this ②_____ to Japan. How much is it using the cheapest ③_____?
Clerk: Twenty dollars by ④_____ mail and thirty dollars by air mail.
Anne: I see. Then by air mail, please.
Clerk: ⑤_____. Could you tell me what's in it?
Anne: It ⑥_____ fragile ⑦_____, so would you handle it with ⑧_____?
Clerk: Sure. Will you ⑨_____ out the form to ⑩_____ them?
Anne: OK. I will.

B 登場人物の名前を自分の名前に置き換えて、パートナーと上の会話を練習しましょう。

💡 Tips for Part 1   被写体の配置をすばやくとらえる

✔ 写真を見て人や物、建物などの配置をすばやくとらえます。音声が流れる前に、できるだけ写真の内容を詳細に見ておくように意識しましょう。また、前置詞 (句) を中心に、配置を表す語句を身につけましょう。

    ex. Two people are chatting over coffee **in front of** the cafeteria.

🎧 Let's Practice

下の名詞と前置詞を使って、写真を描写する文を作りましょう。修飾する語句は自分で付け加えます。人や物の位置に特に注意を払いましょう。

名詞	man	store	clothes	counter
	plants	jackets	sweater	
前置詞	next to	between	on	over
	behind	near	in	

    ex. Various things are arranged on a counter.

1. _____

2. _____

Exercises for Part 1

A 下の写真を描写する4つの英文を聞き、最も適切なものを選びましょう。　🔊 A-56〜57

1.　　　　　　　　　　　　　　　　　　　　2.

　　　Ⓐ Ⓑ Ⓒ Ⓓ　　　　　　　　　　　　　　　Ⓐ Ⓑ Ⓒ Ⓓ

B もう一度聞いて、正しい描写文の最初の5語を書き取りましょう。　🔊 A-56〜57

1. _____ _____ _____ _____ _____

2. _____ _____ _____ _____ _____

Strategies for the Reading Section

📖 Warm-Up Reading　　　　　　　　　　　　　　　🔊 A-58

A 英文を流れに沿って理解し、スピードを意識して速読しましょう。

　Holding a credit card has become a lifestyle for many people. Early credit cards were used in the 1920's in the United States specifically to sell fuel to the growing number of car owners. These cards were accepted only at gas stations belonging to a corporate group in limited locations. About thirty years later, the concept of the modern credit card was said to have been established. Credit cards are very convenient because card holders can purchase goods without cash and pay for them at a later date. They are also convenient for shopping and booking a hotel or a flight online. When shopping online with a credit card, customers only need to enter their address, card number and the card's expiration date. Because credit cards allow more freedom to buy, many people tend to overspend. They must learn how to use their credit cards wisely.

(146 words)　time ＿＿＿　wpm ＿＿＿

B 上の英文の内容に関する質問に英語で答えましょう。

1. For what purpose were early credit cards used?
　_____

2. When was the concept of the modern credit card established?
　_____

3. What problem occurs due to the ease of use of credit cards?
　_____

Grammar Points　｜　時制 (1)　現在進行形

現在進行形 (be動詞＋〜ing) は進行中の動作や状態の他に、現在の時点ですでに計画されている未来のことを表す場合にも用いることができる。特に、arrive、come、go などの往来を表す動詞は、現在進行形を使って未来のことを表す場合が多い。

　現在進行形：*ex.*　The governor **is coming** to our town this week.（未来の出来事）

なお、以下のように「状態」を表す動詞は進行形にならない。

進行形にならない動詞
　知覚・認識の動詞：desire、feel、hate、hear、know、like、remember、see、smell など。
　　　　ex.　My sister **believes** dreams foretell the future.

　関係を表す動詞：belong to、consist of、contain、cost、need、possess、seem など。
　　　　ex.　Jim strongly **resembles** his father.

Unit 5 Purchasing

> **Grammar Quiz**　（　）内の正しい語句を○で囲みましょう。
> 1. That black briefcase (belongs / is belonging) to Professor Smith.
> 2. We (start / are starting) a new advertising campaign some time soon.
> 3. When I arrived home, my mother (prepared / was preparing) dinner in the kitchen.

💡 Tips for Part 6　　主語と述語動詞をしっかり把握する

✔ 空所を含む英文の主部が長い場合、主語となる名詞を把握できるかどうかが、適切な述語動詞を選ぶカギとなります。関係代名詞節がある場合は、関係代名詞が何を指すかを把握することが動詞を選ぶカギとなる問題も出題されます。

✎ Exercises for Part 6

文を完成させるのに、最も適切なものを選びましょう。

Green Box　　Outlet furniture store　　*Spring Sale*

Green Box, one of the finest online furniture stores, ------- furniture online at the most affordable prices. With furnishing options provided by some of the world's leading manufacturers, you can find discount furniture online that ------- a richer look to any environment.
                                                    1.   **2.**

Green Box sales are prime opportunities to perfect your home's personality since our everyday low prices are reduced even further. Take advantage of this by picking up a few accent pillows, a new rug, or some heavily discounted furniture. Although the prices are a fraction of what you'd find anywhere else, furniture discounted during our sales is of the same high quality as all the other pieces found on our site. -------.
                                                                                                3.

---

1. (A) are providing　(B) will provide　(C) provides　(D) provide　　Ⓐ Ⓑ Ⓒ Ⓓ

2. (A) brings　　(B) bringing　　(C) bring　　(D) to bring　　Ⓐ Ⓑ Ⓒ Ⓓ

3. (A) We buy furnishings in large whole sale quantities direct from manufactures.
　　(B) There are so many colors and options to choose from.
　　(C) Many home accessories at Green Box are shipped via UPS Standard Ground shipping.
　　(D) Your guests will be shocked when you tell them how much money you saved at Green Box.
　　　　　　　　　　　　　　　　　　　　　　　　　　　　　　　　Ⓐ Ⓑ Ⓒ Ⓓ

MINI TOEIC L&R TEST

Listening Section

Part 1 Photographs   ◉ A-59

1.

Ⓐ Ⓑ Ⓒ Ⓓ

Part 2 Question-Response   ◉ A-60~62

2. Ⓐ Ⓑ Ⓒ
3. Ⓐ Ⓑ Ⓒ
4. Ⓐ Ⓑ Ⓒ

Part 3 Conversations   ◉ A-63~64

5. What does the woman want to buy?
   - (A) Trousers
   - (B) A sweater
   - (C) A dress
   - (D) A scarf

   Ⓐ Ⓑ Ⓒ Ⓓ

6. What does the woman think is a problem?
   - (A) The sweater is too costly to buy.
   - (B) The red tags are 20% off.
   - (C) The yellow tags aren't marked 20% off.
   - (D) 10% off is good enough.

   Ⓐ Ⓑ Ⓒ Ⓓ

7. Which item of the following is 10% off?
   - (A) Scarves
   - (B) Sweaters
   - (C) Pants
   - (D) Blouses

   Ⓐ Ⓑ Ⓒ Ⓓ

Unit 5 Purchasing   69

Part 4 Talks

🔊 A-65~66

8. What is the purpose of this announcement?
   (A) To introduce nourishing products
   (B) To discount flour
   (C) To show canned soups
   (D) To introduce bargains

9. In which aisle can listeners get French wines and cheeses?
   (A) 1A
   (B) 2B
   (C) 3A
   (D) 3C

10. How much of a discount can listeners get for Italian food?
    (A) 20% off
    (B) 30% off
    (C) 40% off
    (D) 50% off

Reading Section

Part 5 Incomplete Sentences

11. My friend and I ------- some money right away.
    (A) are needing
    (B) need
    (C) had needed
    (D) needing

12. All T-shirts and pants at the store ------- at the reduced prices.
    (A) is offering
    (B) is offered
    (C) are offering
    (D) are offered

13. The popularity of Pike shoes ------- steadily year by year.
    (A) have been increased
    (B) has been increasing
    (C) are increasing
    (D) will be increased

Part 6 Text Completion

Questions 14-16 refer to the following advertisement.

Hill Carlton Moving Sale

Hill Carlton, premier Boston jeweler, announced a moving sale today, which will continue until the end of September. It will temporarily relocate to a storefront location in Parkside Mall in early October, while its new showroom ------- remodeled. The new shop will
14.
be located in the same Parkside Mall but on the second floor and ------- to open in
15.
the middle of October. It will be a more spacious and comfortable area. However, its telephone number and e-mail address remain the same. Every piece of jewelry in the Hill Carlton showroom is on sale for 30% to up to 70% off. -------. This moving sale is a great
16.
opportunity to buy something beautiful and rare that will last a lifetime.

14. (A) being
    (B) be to
    (C) is being
    (D) are

15. (A) scheduled
    (B) is scheduled
    (C) be scheduling
    (D) have scheduled

16. (A) Michael Moore will oversee the interior design of the new showroom.
    (B) Latest fall arrivals, including leaf motifs on rings, are also available at 30% off their retail price.
    (C) Parkside Mall is a three-level shopping center offering over 100 stores.
    (D) The official opening of Hill Carlton's new showroom will take place at the Parkside Mall.

Part 7 Reading Comprehension

Questions 17-20 refer to the following e-mail.

From: Tokyo Books Online
To: Jacob Pasche
Subject: Order Information
Date: May 7

Dear Mr. Pasche:

This e-mail is to inform you that we are in receipt of your order placed on May 5.

Your order confirmation number is MJ-10553. If you have any questions concerning your order, you will be asked to refer to this number. Please print this sheet out and keep it until you receive the book you ordered.

Due to unexpectedly great demand from customers, your order will be delayed by three weeks. When your order is shipped, you will receive an e-mail about the estimated delivery date.

For your convenience, you can track shipment status at www.tokyobooks-online.com. You can also access our chat support system on the Web site or call our customer service center at 002-303-7855, which is open Monday through Saturday from 9:00 A.M. to 6:00 P.M.

Thank you again for your cooperation. We hope you have not been seriously inconvenienced by the delay.

Sincerely,

Margaret Chan
Customer Service Manager
Tokyo Books Online

17. What is the purpose of this message?
    (A) To ask for payment
    (B) To inform the customer the order was accepted
    (C) To respond to a customer complaint
    (D) To report mistakes in the order

    Ⓐ Ⓑ Ⓒ Ⓓ

18. According to the e-mail, why is the order confirmation number important?
    (A) It is the number to identify the customer.
    (B) It is necessary to know the contents of the book.
    (C) It is the number to call for the customer service center.
    (D) It is necessary when the customer makes inquiries.

    Ⓐ Ⓑ Ⓒ Ⓓ

19. When will the book Mr. Pasche ordered probably be shipped?
    (A) On May 5
    (B) On May 7
    (C) In the middle of May
    (D) At the end of May

    Ⓐ Ⓑ Ⓒ Ⓓ

20. What is NOT mentioned as a means of checking shipment status?
    (A) Tracking through a Web site
    (B) Calling the customer service center
    (C) Sending a letter to the company
    (D) Using a chat support system

    Ⓐ Ⓑ Ⓒ Ⓓ

Listening Section /10 | **Reading Section** /10 | **Total** /20

Unit 6
Housing & Accommodations

👍 Vocabulary Builder　　　　　　　　　　　　　　　　　　🔊 A-67

A 語句の品詞と意味を書きましょう。

	品詞	意味		品詞	意味
1. owner	( )	_____	6. financial	( )	_____
2. rent	( )	_____	7. share	( )	_____
3. utilities	( )	_____	8. lease	( )	_____
4. landlady	( )	_____	9. deposit	( )	_____
5. tenant	( )	_____	10. issue	( )	_____

B [ ]内の指示に従って単語を書き換えましょう。

1. owner　　［動詞］⇨ _____　　3. financial　［名詞］⇨ _____
2. tenant　　［反意語］⇨ _____　　4. utility　　［動詞］⇨ _____

Strategies for the Listening Section

🎧 Warm-Up Listening 　　　　　　　　　　　　　　　　　　　　　　🔊 A-68

A アンとマキの会話を聞き、空所を埋めましょう。

Anne: This is a great apartment, Maki. And it's only a ①_____, skip, and a jump to the station. How much rent do you pay for ②_____?

Maki: Only ③_____ a month, plus utilities. My father knows the ④_____. So I can get a discount.

Anne: Wow, that's a ⑤_____! Could I sleep on your couch for a few days?

Maki: More ⑥_____ welcome, Anne. But keep a low ⑦_____, please. My ⑧_____ is pretty strict.

Anne: You bet! I'll be very quiet and keep your place ⑨_____ during my stay.

Maki: ⑩_____!

B 登場人物の名前を自分の名前に置き換えて、パートナーと上の会話を練習しましょう。

💡 Tips for Part 2 　　Yes/No 疑問文は内容をよく理解する

✔ Yes/No 疑問文に対して、実際の会話では Yes や No を使って答えない場合もよくあります。これは応答の内容を直接すばやく伝えるためです。疑問文の細かいポイントをよく聞き取って判断することが大切です。

    ex.   **Q:** Was the negotiation successful?
          A: An agreement is ready to be signed.

✍ Let's Practice

次の各質問に合う応答を a〜d から選びましょう。

1. Are the reports ready to send out? 　　(　　)
2. Do you mind if I open the window? 　　(　　)
3. Was the meeting postponed? 　　(　　)
4. Did you order our letterhead stationery? 　(　　)

> a. Yes, because Mr. Dale hasn't arrived yet.
> b. The delivery should be here tomorrow.
> c. I'm going to the post office right now.
> d. Not at all, go ahead.

Exercises for Part 2

A 質問に対する 3 つの応答を聞き、最も適切なものを選びましょう。　　A-69〜70

1. Ⓐ Ⓑ Ⓒ
2. Ⓐ Ⓑ Ⓒ

B もう一度聞いて、質問の最初の 5 語を書き取りましょう。　　A-69〜70

1. _____ _____ _____ _____ _____

2. _____ _____ _____ _____ _____

Strategies for the Reading Section

Warm-Up Reading   A-71

A 英文を流れに沿って理解し、スピードを意識して速読しましょう。

A roommate relationship is more than a living arrangement. Roommates can have an emotional as well as a financial effect on each other's lives. There are many laws to define the relationship between landlord and tenant but none that deal specifically with roommate relationships. It is important to choose a roommate wisely and to be a good roommate yourself so that you will be able to work out any problems that might occur. If you arrange to share an apartment with a roommate you don't know, ask the landlord to let you sign separate leases so that each of you is responsible only for your share of the rent and any damages you cause. Your best friend may not be the best choice for a roommate. Living together could harm your friendship if you find that you disagree about cleaning, paying bills or other issues that sometimes arise when sharing an apartment.

(152 words)   time [   ]   wpm [   ]

B 上の英文の内容に関する質問に英語で答えましょう。

1. What effect can roommates have on each other's lives?
   _____

2. Why is it important to choose a roommate wisely and to be a good roommate?
   _____

3. What might be a good idea when you decide to share an apartment with a stranger?
   _____

Grammar Points | 時制(2) 過去形・現在完了形

過去形：
- **ex.** He **started** a business of his own three years ago.（過去の動作や状態）
- In those days, people here **went** to the market every weekend.（過去の習慣）
- The party **ended** before I got there.（過去完了の代用）
- ＊before や after など接続詞で時間の前後関係が明らかな場合には過去形を用いる。

現在完了形：過去の動作や状態が、何らかのかたちで現在とつながりがあることを表す。
- **ex.** I **have** just **finished** my work.（完了）
- ＊just、now、already、yet、recently などの副詞を伴うことが多い。
- **ex.** **Have** you ever **used** a mobile phone?（現在までの経験）
- ＊ever、never、once、before などの副詞を伴うことが多い。
- **ex.** We **have lived** here for nearly 30 years.（現在までの状態の継続）

Grammar Quiz （　）内の正しい語句を○で囲みましょう。

1. They asked me to fill out the form in the same way as I (did / had done) before.
2. We (were researching / have been researching) the Chinese market since last year.
3. The computer I (bought / have bought) three months ago is already broken.

Tips for Part 7　5W1Hに注目する・文挿入問題

✔ Part 7で出題される記事や告知文は、全体の内容をすばやくつかむために、5W1H（who、when、where、what、why、how）に当たる情報を読み取る必要があります。文挿入問題では、挿入文に代名詞がある場合、it や they が指すものが何か、空所の前の文から把握しましょう。段落がある場合は、各段落の最初の1、2文から内容を素早く把握し、挿入文と関係のある段落を見つけましょう。次のExercisesのパッセージを5W1Hに注意しながら読んでみましょう。

Exercises for Part 7

次の告知文を読み、質問に答えましょう。

Hardman Homes has joined in partnership with local landlords and our contractors to hold a DIY workshop for tenants. —[1]—. The workshop is on Thursday, July 5 from 9:30 A.M. to 12:30 P.M. at the South Bay Center, St Luke's Way. —[2]—.

Interactive workshops will run continuously throughout the session and cover a wide range of common household tasks including: a) tiling, sealing and grouting, b) hanging wallpaper, c) painting doors and walls, d) plumbing tips, and e) how to use power tools. —[3]—.

These workshops can prepare you with knowledge, experience and skills so you can tackle these jobs yourself. To book a place, please contact Hardman Homes at 592-3946. —[4]—. We look forward to seeing you there.

---

1. What is the purpose of the notice?
   (A) To announce the two companies' merger
   (B) To invite house and apartment residents to a company event
   (C) To introduce new power tools to real estate tenants
   (D) To explain the importance of DIY　　　　　　Ⓐ Ⓑ Ⓒ Ⓓ

2. In which of the positions marked [1], [2], [3], and [4] does the following sentence best belong?

   "If you are a tenant of Hardman Family Condominiums, please call the manager's office."
   (A) [1]
   (B) [2]
   (C) [3]
   (D) [4]　　　　　　Ⓐ Ⓑ Ⓒ Ⓓ

MINI TOEIC L&R TEST

Listening Section

Part 1 Photographs   A-72

1.

Ⓐ Ⓑ Ⓒ Ⓓ

Part 2 Question-Response   A-73~75

2. Ⓐ Ⓑ Ⓒ
3. Ⓐ Ⓑ Ⓒ
4. Ⓐ Ⓑ Ⓒ

Part 3 Conversations   A-76~77

5. What is the woman's concern?
   (A) Noisy neighbors
   (B) Finding a new tenant
   (C) Her annual income
   (D) Paying more rent
   Ⓐ Ⓑ Ⓒ Ⓓ

6. When might the rent go up?
   (A) Next January
   (B) Next April
   (C) Next June
   (D) Next August
   Ⓐ Ⓑ Ⓒ Ⓓ

7. Who is the man going to ask the question to?
   (A) His neighbors
   (B) His landlord
   (C) His friends
   (D) His colleagues
   Ⓐ Ⓑ Ⓒ Ⓓ

Unit 6 Housing & Accommodations

Part 4 Talks 🔊 A-78~79

8. What is being announced?
   (A) A new restaurant
   (B) A community project
   (C) A county sports festival
   (D) A picnic in the district
   Ⓐ Ⓑ Ⓒ Ⓓ

9. What will be provided by the day before the event?
   (A) Dinner
   (B) Lunch
   (C) Garbage bags
   (D) Champagne
   Ⓐ Ⓑ Ⓒ Ⓓ

10. When will the event be postponed to if it rains?
    (A) This Sunday
    (B) This Saturday
    (C) This Friday
    (D) Next Saturday
    Ⓐ Ⓑ Ⓒ Ⓓ

Reading Section

Part 5 Incomplete Sentences

11. The Hawk Real Estate Agency ------- 30 new men and women in 2018.
    (A) has employed
    (B) had employed
    (C) employed
    (D) employs
    Ⓐ Ⓑ Ⓒ Ⓓ

12. My sister and I were separated after the war and I ------- her for 15 years.
    (A) didn't see
    (B) don't see
    (C) haven't seen
    (D) am not seeing
    Ⓐ Ⓑ Ⓒ Ⓓ

13. I paid a pet deposit and ------- a pet agreement before moving into a new apartment.
    (A) have signed
    (B) signed
    (C) sign
    (D) signing
    Ⓐ Ⓑ Ⓒ Ⓓ

Part 6 Text Completion

Questions 14-16 refer to the following advertisement.

Scot Company Real Estate

Scot Company Real Estate was established by Kathryn A. Scot in 1986. The company has provided superior services that help clients buy or lease their ideal property and ------- (14.) their real estate assets for over 30 years. Through expertise, service and integrity, the company's goal is to exceed every client's expectations. ------- (15.). We have put together a collaborative team of licensed professionals who work together to achieve a higher level of client satisfaction.

If you are looking to buy or lease a property, you can search our database by location, price, and size. Once you ------- (16.) down your top choices, our agents can help with the rest.

14. (A) will sell
    (B) sells
    (C) sold
    (D) sell

15. (A) We run each property as an individual business.
    (B) We serve the downtown area with commercial real estate and property management services.
    (C) We live, work and play in the neighborhoods we sell.
    (D) We offer real estate agent services that include representation for buyers, sellers, and tenants.

16. (A) will narrow
    (B) would narrow
    (C) have narrowed
    (D) had narrowed

Part 7 Reading Comprehension

Questions 17-18 refer to the following advertisement.

Golden Valley, California

National Magazine Names Golden Valley In Top 20!

New Choices for Retirement Living Style magazine has selected Golden Valley among the very best in the nation from 1,500 retirement communities surveyed. They said "it is the highest value for your retirement dollar." Choose from 8 model units and 23 amazing floor plan choices with square footage ranging from 1,200 to 3,000 square feet.

It's a small town with shopping, medical facilities, places of worship and lots of friendly neighbors.

Golf Plus A Lot More!

Golden Valley's multi-million dollar recreation complex includes the best in resort enjoyments: ◆ Five Golf Courses ◆ 2-Story Clubhouse ◆ Health Club ◆ Arts & Crafts ◆ Four Tennis Courts ◆ Pools & Jacuzzis ◆ Dining, Lounge & More.

Model units open daily 9 A.M.- 6 P.M. Take I-20 east of Lafayette to Exit 52. California: 612-3335 Out of State: 1-800-634-5788

17. For whom is this information intended?
    (A) Golf lovers of all ages
    (B) Young families with children
    (C) Those who will live on pensions
    (D) Those who like shopping
    Ⓐ Ⓑ Ⓒ Ⓓ

18. What is indicated about Golden Valley?
    (A) It offers eight house model units in the same size.
    (B) Its model units are open 9 A.M. - 6 P.M. every day.
    (C) It has five golf courses and two clubhouses.
    (D) It owns out-of-state facilities.
    Ⓐ Ⓑ Ⓒ Ⓓ

Questions 19-20 refer to the following information.

WELCOME TO SKY VIEW!

Welcome to your new home. It is our intention to operate and maintain the community in which you now live as one of the outstanding communities in the Brownsville area. Please read the booklet. We hope it will be an aid to you in enjoying your new home.

TELEPHONE NUMBERS:

On-Site Manager	622-3535	Property Mgmt Office	881-7676
US West Telephone	670-8811	Northwest Gas	995-1888
Water and Sewer	792-3446		

OCCUPANCY LIMITS:

There is a limit on the number of people allowed to occupy your home. A limited number of guests may stay with you for three days. After three days, we may assume they are residents. If you find a need to have more people living in your home than allowed by your lease, contact the manager to see if it can be allowed. Having more people than allowed is a violation of your rental agreement. You may incur additional charges and/or have your rental agreement terminated.

19. For whom is this information intended?

    (A) The manager of the apartment
    (B) A real estate agent
    (C) A resident of the apartment
    (D) A person staying at the apartment temporarily

20. Which of the following statements is true about the occupancy limit?

    (A) You have to receive an entrance permit for your guests.
    (B) You must renew the rental agreement in a week.
    (C) Your guests are regarded as residents when a certain period has passed.
    (D) Your guests can stay with you for more than four days.

Unit 7
Office Work (1)

Vocabulary Builder　　　　　　　　　　　　　　　　　　　　　　A-80

A 語句の品詞と意味を書きましょう。

　　　　　　　　　品詞　　　意味　　　　　　　　　　　　　品詞　　　意味

1. quantity 　　　(　　) _____　6. wrap 　　(　　) _____
2. state-of-the-art (　　) _____　7. aisle 　　(　　) _____
3. reputation 　　(　　) _____　8. range 　　(　　) _____
4. reduction 　　(　　) _____　9. cashier 　(　　) _____
5. negotiate 　　(　　) _____　10. clerk 　　(　　) _____

B [ ]内の指示に従って単語を書き換えましょう。

1. quantity　　[反意語] ⇨ _____　3. reduction　[動詞] ⇨ _____
2. reputation　[同義語] ⇨ _____　4. negotiate　[名詞] ⇨ _____

Strategies for the Listening Section

🎧 Warm-Up Listening   ◀))A-81

A ウィルとケンの会話を聞き、空所を埋めましょう。

Will: Ken, I hear that video games are ①_____ in Japan.
Ken: Yes, ②_____ of various generations can enjoy ③_____.
Will: Our products are selling in large ④_____ in the U.S. And the ⑤_____ video game has a good ⑥_____ among many customers.
Ken: We believe the game you're talking about ⑦_____ to Japanese, too. What is the ⑧_____ price?
Will: We can offer you this item at $35 ⑨_____ unit.
Ken: What about price reduction? I believe there's a chance we can ⑩_____.

B 登場人物の名前を自分の名前に置き換えて、パートナーと上の会話を練習しましょう。

💡 Tips for Part 3   連結音に耳を慣らしておく

✔ 自然な会話の中では2つの単語が連結して発音に変化が起きることがよくあります。これはリンキングと呼ばれるもので、文章中で特定の単語の末尾の語と直後の単語の最初の音が連結して違う発音になります。

例えば、in front of、tell her、good afternoon、kind of などのように、前の単語の末尾の子音と直後の単語の母音や弱音がつながって発音されるときに起こります。細心の注意をして音を聞き取りましょう。

🎧 Let's Practice   ◀))A-82

次の音声を聞いて、最初の4語を書き取りましょう。

1. _____ _____ _____ _____ the bush, Boss.

2. _____ _____ _____ _____ in the near future.

3. _____ _____ _____ _____ will pass the entrance exam.

Unit 7 Office Work (1)

Exercises for Part 3

会話を聞いて、質問に対する正しい答えを選びましょう。　　　A-83

1. What is the problem?
   - (A) The woman is sick.
   - (B) The woman is late for work.
   - (C) The woman is too busy.
   - (D) The woman can't get to sleep.

   Ⓐ Ⓑ Ⓒ Ⓓ

2. What is the man's advice?
   - (A) To work at home
   - (B) To see a doctor
   - (C) To take medicine
   - (D) To rest in bed

   Ⓐ Ⓑ Ⓒ Ⓓ

Strategies for the Reading Section

📖 Warm-Up Reading 🔊 A-84

A 英文を流れに沿って理解し、スピードを意識して速読しましょう。

Nowadays, self-service chain grocery stores are popular. The world's first self-service grocery store was established in 1916 in Memphis, in the United States. Until then, grocery stores gave full service. Shop staff standing at the counter got products from shelves for customers. As many food items were not individually wrapped for family or single use, a store clerk had to measure and wrap the items for each customer. These stores usually carried only one brand of each of the goods. The self-service grocery stores and the supermarkets which first opened in 1930 changed this style. Shoppers now walk along the aisles between the shelves filled with a wide range of goods. They select their goods and then go to the checkout line to have a cashier check their orders out. The self-service stores can not only give customers quicker service but lower labor costs.

(144 words)　time [　　]　wpm [　　]

B 上の英文の内容に関する質問に英語で答えましょう。

1. What is the article mainly about?
   _____

2. How are full-service and self-service grocery stores different?
   _____

3. What are the advantages of self-service stores?
   _____

Grammar Points　動名詞と不定詞

目的語をとる動詞の中には、to不定詞をとる動詞、動名詞をとる動詞、to不定詞と動名詞のどちらもとる動詞がある。

to不定詞を目的語にとる動詞：aim、arrange、decide、expect、hope、manage、offer、pretend、promise、refuseなど。

　ex. He **agreed to sell** his car at such a low price.

動名詞を目的語にとる動詞：admit、appreciate、deny、escape、finish、mind、quit、give up、put offなど。

　ex. I **postponed going** to the dentist.

どちらも目的語にとる動詞：remember、forget、try、regretなど。

　ex. Please **remember to call** our client.（忘れないで～する）
　　　 I **remember meeting** him once before.（～したことを覚えている）

Grammar Quiz （　）内の正しい語句を○で囲みましょう。

1. The instruction manual was so complicated that I stopped (to read / reading) it.
2. The employees disliked (to work / working) late every day.
3. We made many plans for the weekend, but ended up (to stay / staying) at home.

Tips for Part 5　　句動詞を身につける

✔ make、take、look、do などの動詞が前置詞や副詞を伴ってできたフレーズを句動詞と言います。これらの動詞は前置詞や副詞を切り離すと意味をなさないので、前置詞や副詞に注意して句動詞を身につけることが語彙力の向上につながります。Part 5 では、句動詞を選択する場合と句動詞の一部である動詞または前置詞の選択を問うものが出題されます。

Exercises for Part 5

文を完成させるのに、最も適切なものを選びましょう。

1. The manager has promised that she will look ------- the customer's complaint at once.
   (A) out　　　(B) on　　　(C) into　　　(D) forward

2. Just as the burglar thought he was safely inside the shop, the alarm -------.
   (A) took off　　　(B) went off　　　(C) turned down　　　(D) put in

3. We should ------- equipment when leaving the office.
   (A) put away　　　(B) make out　　　(C) hit upon　　　(D) move in

4. John decided to ------- his father's business after working for the company for a few years.
   (A) call off　　　(B) look over　　　(C) cut down　　　(D) take over

5. The mechanic could not figure ------- what was wrong with the engine.
   (A) for　　　(B) in　　　(C) on　　　(D) out

MINI TOEIC L&R TEST

Listening Section

Part 1 Photographs 🔊 A-85

1.

Ⓐ Ⓑ Ⓒ Ⓓ

Part 2 Question-Response 🔊 A-86~88

2. Ⓐ Ⓑ Ⓒ
3. Ⓐ Ⓑ Ⓒ
4. Ⓐ Ⓑ Ⓒ

Part 3 Conversations 🔊 A-89~90

5. Where most likely are the speakers?
   (A) In a bookstore
   (B) In a conference room
   (C) In a library
   (D) At a reception desk
   Ⓐ Ⓑ Ⓒ Ⓓ

6. What will probably happen in April?
   (A) Each of the speakers will start researching the e-book market.
   (B) The manager is going to give a demo lesson.
   (C) Consumers will purchase recent magazine issues.
   (D) Their product will change the old-fashioned reading style.
   Ⓐ Ⓑ Ⓒ Ⓓ

7. What does the man mean when he says, "it's nothing personal"?
   (A) He doesn't wish to offend her.
   (B) He means there is a personal reason.
   (C) He is surprised to see her puzzled face.
   (D) He shifts the responsibility to her.
   Ⓐ Ⓑ Ⓒ Ⓓ

Unit 7 Office Work (1)

Part 4 Talks

8. What is being announced?
   (A) The company's revenues
   (B) The selection of chiefs
   (C) The presentation of an award
   (D) The growth of a group

9. How often is the event held?
   (A) Once every two years
   (B) Once in three years
   (C) Once in a while
   (D) Once a year

10. How much did the earnings reach by the end of 2018?
    (A) $12 million
    (B) $20 million
    (C) $2 billion
    (D) $22 billion

Reading Section

Part 5 Incomplete Sentences

11. The man denied ------- hundreds of credit card numbers and other personal information belonging to clients of his company.
    (A) to have stolen
    (B) having stolen
    (C) has stolen
    (D) stole

12. When the manager asked Lisa to work overtime, she politely ------- his request.
    (A) got through
    (B) turned down
    (C) taken apart
    (D) made up

13. Pam asked the shop clerk whether she could ------- the suit displayed in the window.
    (A) bring up
    (B) look into
    (C) take off
    (D) try on

Part 6 Text Completion

Questions 14-16 refer to the following notice.

To All New Employees of SKD Foods

Welcome to SKD Foods. The parking ------- applies to all employees. A few parking spaces are ------- for executives and employees who drive company vehicles. We'll allocate our remaining parking spaces according to the following priorities: 1) disabled employees and pregnant women, 2) night shift workers, 3) other full-time and part-time employees whose commuting distance is more than three miles. Employees whose commuting distance is less than three miles can purchase a parking permit on request and at a cost of $50 per year, but space is limited. -------. For further information, please contact Kent Peters at the parking office.

14. (A) law
    (B) policy
    (C) politics
    (D) administration

15. (A) set aside
    (B) looked into
    (C) put off
    (D) carried on

16. (A) It is a convenient location to meet visitors.
    (B) We expect drivers to maintain a clean and safe parking space.
    (C) No employee will be eligible to purchase more than one parking permit.
    (D) All employees are required to wear ID badges while on SKD Foods property.

Part 7   Reading Comprehension

Questions 17-20 refer to the following notice.

To all employees,

Don't forget to renew your security cards. These are valid for 3 years and most of you will have to renew them by September 5. —[1]—.
Please submit your current security cards to the General Affairs Department. Cards can be requested from 2:00 to 5:00 in the afternoon, Monday through Friday. The renewal process takes less than an hour. If your card is not renewed by September 5, your access to this building will be denied. —[2]—.

Damaged Cards: If you have a damaged card, turn it in and a new one will be issued to replace it. —[3]—. If it can be proved that the card was deliberately damaged, a charge of $10 will be applied, irrespective of whether this is the first replacement or not.

Lost or Stolen Cards: If you lost your card, please contact Susan Walter ext. 4050 as soon as possible so we can deactivate your card. After your card is deactivated, you must come to the General Affairs Department to receive a new security card. Please bring one form of personal identification (e.g., driving license, bank card, etc.). You do not need to bring a photo. The department will take your photograph before your card is issued. —[4]—. If your card was lost or stolen, you will be charged a replacement card fee of $20.

17. To whom is this notice addressed?
    (A) All members of the staff
    (B) All staff members of the General Affairs Department
    (C) Most of the staff members in the company
    (D) Most of the staff members in the Security Department

18. What should employees do if their card is lost or stolen?
    (A) They should call a person in charge immediately.
    (B) They have to pay $10 to get a new card.
    (C) They must bring their photo.
    (D) They have to show two forms of personal identification.

19. The word "deliberately" in paragraph 2, line 2, is closest in meaning to
    (A) primarily
    (B) occasionally
    (C) on purpose
    (D) by chance

20. In which of the positions marked [1], [2], [3], and [4] does the following sentence best belong?

    "In that case, you will need to sign in at the reception desk."

    (A) [1]
    (B) [2]
    (C) [3]
    (D) [4]

Unit 8
Office Work (2)

👍 Vocabulary Builder   🔊 B-02

A 語句の品詞と意味を書きましょう。

	品詞	意味		品詞	意味
1. ship	( )	_____	6. complaint	( )	_____
2. delivery	( )	_____	7. positive	( )	_____
3. apparently	( )	_____	8. courteously	( )	_____
4. mention	( )	_____	9. identify	( )	_____
5. intend	( )	_____	10. exchange	( )	_____

B [ ]内の指示に従って単語を書き換えましょう。

1. ship　　　　［名詞］⇨ _____　　3. identify　［名詞］⇨ _____
2. delivery　　［動詞］⇨ _____　　4. positive　［反意語］⇨ _____

94

Strategies for the Listening Section

🎧 Warm-Up Listening 🔊 B-03

A ケンとウィルの電話での会話を聞き、空所を埋めましょう。

Ken: Hi, Mr. Wilson. We had ①_____ 3,000 of the "Trap Game" and
②_____ of the "Maze Game," but they were shipped ③_____.

Will: I'll check with our delivery ④_____. Just a moment please.
A few minutes later
Hello, thank you for waiting.

Ken: Hello, so, ⑤_____ happened?

Will: OK, this is what happened. There's been a mix-up at the ⑥_____ company.
⑦_____, they had a ⑧_____ delivery scheduled.

Ken: I understand. Next time, please send us the products we ordered ⑨_____.

Will: Yes. I'll make sure. I hope we'll still have a good ⑩_____ after this.

B 登場人物の名前を自分の名前に置き換えて、パートナーと上の会話を練習しましょう。

💡 *Tips for Part 4*　説明文が流れる前に図表を確認し、質問文を速読する

✔ 説明文が流れる前に図表を確認し、3問の質問文をすばやく読破しましょう。その際、キーワードだけを速読すると確実です。質問文の最初の疑問詞だけでも、もう一度目を通しましょう。

✔ "Look at the graphic." で始まる設問は、説明文の内容と図表 (リスト、スケジュール表、地図など) の情報を関連付けて答えましょう。スケジュール変更などの内容を伴うことも多いので、会話の展開を最後までよく聞いて判断しましょう。

🎧 *Let's Practice*

太字のキーワードだけを見て質問文の意味を推測し、パートナーと確認しましょう。

> *ex.* **How** did **the speaker get** to the **museum**?
> ⇨「どうやって　話し手は着く（着いた）　美術館に？」

1. **Where** would this **message** be **heard**?
   ⇨ _____

2. **What** will **tomorrow's** local **weather** be?
   ⇨ _____

Exercises for Part 4

A 先に表と質問文の太字部分だけを読み、その後で説明文を聞いて、正しい答えを選びましょう。　B-04

Shift 1	9:00 A.M. — 4:00 P.M.
Shift 2	11:00 A.M. — 7:00 P.M.
Shift 3	10:00 A.M. — 2:00 P.M.
Shift 4	3:00 P.M. — 8:00 P.M.

1. **Who** is the **speaker** probably **talking to**?

    (A) Candidates
    (B) Regular employees
    (C) Club members
    (D) Customers

    Ⓐ Ⓑ Ⓒ Ⓓ

2. Look at the **graphic**. **How long** is **Group A** of the **additional workers** going to **work a day**?

    (A) 4 hours
    (B) 5 hours
    (C) 7 hours
    (D) 8 hours

    Ⓐ Ⓑ Ⓒ Ⓓ

B 説明文の一部をもう一度聞いて、（　）に適語を入れましょう。　B-05

This is important information from the (① _____), Mr. Jones. We've decided to (② _____) two groups of additional workers to work new shifts. They will work (③ _____) days a week. Workers on our regular (④ _____) to 4:00 and 11:00 to (⑤ _____) shifts will be unaffected.

Strategies for the Reading Section

📖 Warm-Up Reading   🔊 B-06

A 英文を流れに沿って理解し、スピードを意識して速読しましょう。

Dealing with customer complaints is a necessary thing in any business in order to maintain positive customer relationships. The first thing you must do is to listen to the customer courteously. If the customer is very angry, he or she may not state clearly what the problem is. So, you need to practice reading between the lines. Identifying the exact problem will not only help you with that particular customer, but will also help avoid more complaints in the future. Then, ask the customer what he or she would like you to do. Some want their money back and others would be satisfied with an exchange. When a customer complains, it is always necessary to apologize to the customer. No company enjoys listening to customer complaints, but complaints give you a chance to learn how to improve your business.

(139 words) time ☐ wpm ☐

B 上の英文の内容に関する質問に英語で答えましょう。

1. Why can't some customers state their problems clearly?
   _____

2. What should you do when you listen to a customer's complaints?
   _____

3. If a customer is not satisfied with the item he or she bought, what can a shop clerk do?
   _____

Grammar Points 似た意味を持つ前置詞

by / till: byは「〜までに」と動作や状態が「完了」する期限を表し、tillは「〜までずっと」と動作や状態が「継続」する期限を表す。
- ex. I can **finish typing** it **by** four o'clock.（4時までにタイプし終える：完了）
- I'll **wait** here **till** four o'clock.（4時までずっと待つ：継続）

in / within: 未来のことを言う場合、inは「現在から〜後に」という時間の経過を表し、withinは「〜以内に」という一定の期間内を表す。
- ex. I'll call you back **in** a few minutes.（今から数分後に）
- We'll get there **within** an hour.（1時間以内に）

for / during: 「〜の間」と言う場合、forは継続する期間を表し、duringは特定の期間を表す。
- ex. I'll stay in Chicago **for** a week.（1週間）
- We received 200 orders **during** the week.（その週の間）

Grammar Quiz （　）内の正しい語を○で囲みましょう。

1. The boss will come back to the office (for / in) a few minutes.
2. The tennis match has been put off (by / until) next Sunday.
3. The world population could reach 10 billion (by / in) the end of this century.

Tips for Part 6　空所を含む文の前後の文に注目する

✓ 選択肢に接続詞や接続副詞がある場合には、前後の2つの文の関係を把握しましょう。また、選択肢に代名詞がある場合には、空所を含む文の中に代名詞を指すものがないことが多いので、その前までに記述された内容から代名詞が何を指すのかをすばやく見つけましょう。

Exercises for Part 6

文を完成させるのに、最も適切なものを選びましょう。

Dear Mr. Charles,

We regret to have to complain about late delivery of the facial cream and cologne we ordered from you on 15 July. Although you have given us guarantee in delivery within two weeks, we haven't received ------- yet. -------. We must ask you to complete the
　　　　　　　　　　　　　　　　　　 1.　　　　　　 2.
order immediately. -------, we shall have no option but to cancel it and obtain the toiletries
　　　　　　　　　　 3.
elsewhere.

We feel there must be some explanation for this delay and await your prompt reply.

Yours faithfully,

Esmeralda Mendoza

1. (A) some　　(B) you　　(C) them　　(D) one

2. (A) We will return them at your expense.
   (B) We understand that it will take an extra two weeks.
   (C) We have decided to reject this order.
   (D) We are very unhappy with this delay in delivery.

3. (A) Otherwise　(B) However　(C) Therefore　(D) For example

MINI TOEIC L&R TEST

Listening Section

Part 1 Photographs 🔊 B-07

1.

Ⓐ Ⓑ Ⓒ Ⓓ

Part 2 Question-Response 🔊 B-08~10

2. Ⓐ Ⓑ Ⓒ
3. Ⓐ Ⓑ Ⓒ
4. Ⓐ Ⓑ Ⓒ

Part 3 Conversations 🔊 B-11~12

5. What is the woman probably going to do next?
   (A) Go through with the project
   (B) Include the engineers
   (C) Inform others about the meeting
   (D) Call the customers
   Ⓐ Ⓑ Ⓒ Ⓓ

6. Who is attending the meeting?
   (A) The personnel staff
   (B) The managers and the sales staff
   (C) The design programmers
   (D) The computer programmers
   Ⓐ Ⓑ Ⓒ Ⓓ

7. Who most likely is the man?
   (A) Alice's subordinate
   (B) Alice's boss
   (C) Alice's close friend
   (D) Alice's roommate
   Ⓐ Ⓑ Ⓒ Ⓓ

Part 4 Talks

Name	Availability
Mr. Carter	All day Wed. & Thur.
Ms. Klein	All morning Thur. and Fri.
Ms. Wilson	Before 12 P.M. Wed. & Thur.

8. Where is the speaker going to visit this coming Sunday?

   (A) An affiliate
   (B) A trade fair
   (C) An exposition
   (D) A workshop

9. What is the topic the speaker is planning to discuss?

   (A) Time management
   (B) Financial problems
   (C) Human resource management
   (D) Personnel transfers

10. Look at the graphic. When is the most appropriate day for the meeting?

    (A) Monday
    (B) Wednesday
    (C) Thursday
    (D) Friday

Reading Section

Part 5 Incomplete Sentences

11. The manager looked into the causes of the quarrel ------- staff members.

    (A) by
    (B) toward
    (C) in
    (D) among

12. You must make payments ------- 15 days from the date of invoice.

    (A) for
    (B) within
    (C) on
    (D) by

13. Customer satisfaction is very important to us, and ------- we apologize for the inconvenience.

    (A) however
    (B) therefore
    (C) instead
    (D) otherwise

Part 6 Text Completion

Questions 14-16 refer to the following e-mail.

From: Katherine Matthews
To: Greenville Wellness Center
Date: April 21
Subject: Problem in the center

Dear Sir/Madam,

I have been a member of the Greenville Wellness Center for the past five years, ------- 14. I recently found some areas of the center that I will no longer visit because of its poor maintenance. I have noticed that the cleaning of the facilities and equipment has gone down in standard ------- 15. the past couple of months. ------- 16. Its floors have become grimy. I would like to retain membership in the center, but I also want to get good value for my money.

I look forward to hearing from you regarding the resolution to this problem.

Sincerely Yours,

Katherine Matthews

14. (A) because
    (B) but
    (C) when
    (D) or

15. (A) in
    (B) from
    (C) since
    (D) over

16. (A) The fitness facilities help me achieve my goals.
    (B) The shower room is especially bad.
    (C) I have been happy with the clean facilities.
    (D) I need to call your attention to the poor condition of the equipment.

Part 7 Reading Comprehension

Questions 17-20 refer to the following invoice and e-mail.

Hirsch Vineyard, Inc.
www.hirschvineyard.com

Address: Hirsch Vineyard Los Angeles Office
163 Cross Keys Road,
Los Angeles, CA 90045

Invoice #: 45LV20   **Date Invoiced:** May 6
Date Shipped: May 8

Phone: (322) 424-1055

Bill To: Christopher Owen
2534 East 12th Avenue
San Francisco, CA 94120

Ship To: Olive Garden
2530 East 12th Avenue
San Francisco, CA 94120

Item No.	Description	Case Size	Cases	Price/Case	Total
12CB	2012 Chateau Batailley	12 x 750ml	2	$240	$480
10HM	2010 Haut Medoc	12 x 750ml	2	$210	$420
08CN	2008 Carinena	12 x 750ml	1	$300	$300

Comments or Special Instructions:		
*Payment due in 14 days	Sub Total	$1,200
*Please include the invoice number on your check.	Discount	0%
	Tax	$161.70
	Shipping	$90
	Total	**$1,451.70**

Thank you for your business!

Please make all checks payable to Hirsch Vineyard, Inc.

From: Christopher Owen
To: James Martin
Date: May 11
Subject: Invoice #45LV20

Dear Mr. Martin,

The shipment you sent arrived today in good condition. As always, we appreciate your thoughtfulness.

However, the total amount on the invoice doesn't match that on your estimate of May 2. Your invoice does not include a discount of the item No.08CN. We ordered one case because you offered a 30% discount on case purchases of this item. If a discount is not possible, we would like to return this item. The original price of this item does not match the cost of our dishes since we serve casual Italian food with quality wine at affordable prices.

We ask that the error be corrected immediately. Please contact us anytime at 556-3211.

Yours sincerely,
Christopher Owen

17. What is NOT included in the invoice?

    (A) Taxation amounts
    (B) The price per bottle
    (C) An invoice number
    (D) A payment method

    Ⓐ Ⓑ Ⓒ Ⓓ

18. When did Mr. Owen receive the items?

    (A) May 2
    (B) May 6
    (C) May 8
    (D) May 11

    Ⓐ Ⓑ Ⓒ Ⓓ

19. Why was the e-mail sent?

    (A) To inquire about a shipping date
    (B) To advertise the restaurant
    (C) To report a problem with a payment
    (D) To complain about the contents

    Ⓐ Ⓑ Ⓒ Ⓓ

20. In the e-mail, the word "affordable" in paragraph 2, line 5, is closest in meaning to

    (A) modest
    (B) expensive
    (C) ample
    (D) competitive

    Ⓐ Ⓑ Ⓒ Ⓓ

| Listening Section | /10 | Reading Section | /10 | Total | /20 |

Unit 9
Employment

Vocabulary Builder 　　　　　　　　　　　　　　　　　　　　　　　　B-15

A 語句の品詞と意味を書きましょう。

　　　　　　　　　品詞　　　意味　　　　　　　　　　　　　　品詞　　　意味

1. résumé　　　（　　）_____　　6. supervision　（　　）_____
2. vacancy　　 （　　）_____　　7. consistently （　　）_____
3. absolutely　（　　）_____　　8. capacity　　 （　　）_____
4. cell phone　（　　）_____　　9. recommend　　（　　）_____
5. reference　 （　　）_____　 10. apply for　　　　　　_____

B [　] 内の指示に従って単語を書き換えましょう。

1. vacancy　　［形容詞］⇨ _____　　3. apply　　　　［名詞］⇨ _____
2. reference　［動詞］⇨ _____　　　4. supervision　［動詞］⇨ _____

104

Strategies for the Listening Section

🎧 Warm-Up Listening   ◉ B-16

A ウィルとメグの電話での会話を聞き、空所を埋めましょう。

Will: Hello, this is Will Watson calling from the IBS Institute in New York. How are you, Miss Graham?
Meg: Oh, hello. I'm ① _____.
Will: I'm calling because I ② _____ your ③ _____. We're looking for ④ _____ at the moment.
Meg: Really? Thank you for calling.
Will: We have a ⑤ _____ for the position of computer ⑥ _____. We're ⑦ _____ a bunch of people. Is it possible for you to come ⑧ _____ and have a talk with us?
Meg: ⑨ _____! I'll be on my way ⑩ _____ now.

B 登場人物の名前を自分の名前に置き換えて、パートナーと上の会話を練習しましょう。

💡 Tips for Part 1   周りの状況をすばやくチェックする

✔ 複数の人物が描写されている写真の場合、中心人物以外のものが判断材料となることもあります。中心人物だけではなく、周辺の人や物にも注意して状況を判断しましょう。

🎧 Let's Practice

次の質問に英語で答えましょう。

1. 中心人物たちの服装と持ち物について書きなさい。
   _____
   _____

2. それ以外の物について書きなさい。
   _____
   _____

Unit 9 Employment   105

Exercises for Part 1

A 下の写真を描写する4つの英文を聞き、最も適切なものを選びましょう。　🔊 B-17

1.
2.

Ⓐ Ⓑ Ⓒ Ⓓ　　　　　　　　　　　　Ⓐ Ⓑ Ⓒ Ⓓ

B もう一度聞いて、正しい描写文の最初の5語を書き取りましょう。　🔊 B-17

1. _____ _____ _____ _____ _____

2. _____ _____ _____ _____ _____

106

Strategies for the Reading Section

📖 Warm-Up Reading   🔊 B-18

A 英文を流れに沿って理解し、スピードを意識して速読しましょう。

Dear Ms. Carter,

　I am pleased to provide a reference for John Smith for the position of Career Adviser with Sunbury University. John has been working part-time under my supervision for the past six years as a career counseling staff member of South Hill College. There he provides students with on-the-spot advising, directing them to the most appropriate resources (workshops, forums or fairs, etc.) and answering questions. He also conducts one-on-one hour-long consultations with respect to students' career and work options, résumés and cover letters, and interview skills. He works without need for supervision and has demonstrated good judgment consistently in a variety of contexts. He is also highly regarded by his co-workers for his strong teamwork and leadership skills. I highly recommend him for the position for which he has applied. If you require further information regarding John, please feel free to call me.

(145 words) | time | | wpm |

B 上の英文の内容に関する質問に英語で答えましょう。

1. What is the purpose of this letter?

2. Where does John work?

3. How does John help students at work?

Grammar Points　注意すべき比較表現

the ＋比較級～, the ＋比較級 …「～すればするほど、ますます…だ」

　ex. **The more** I know, **the more** I realize that I am ignorant.

superior (inferior / senior / junior) + to …「…よりも優れて (劣って／年上で／年下で)」

　ex. Japanese cars are **superior to** American cars in many ways.

… times as ＋原級＋ as ～「～の…倍」

　ex. Our new office is **three times as large as** our old one.

Grammar Quiz　（　）内の正しい語を○で囲みましょう。

1. My secretary works more (efficient / efficiently) than she used to.
2. He was (superior / better) to any other candidate in organizational skills.
3. The (busiest / busier) you are, the more you need to exercise.

Tips for Part 7　未知語にとらわれないで読み進める・質問形式に慣れる

✔ 意味のわからない単語にとらわれると、読む速度が遅くなってしまいます。前後の文脈や全体の内容から単語の意味を推測しながら、読み進めましょう。

ex. The garbage in and around the city keeps piling up. Yesterday the city government announced plans for a solution including the building of two new incinerators.

※下線部 incinerators の意味を garbage、solution、building などから推測してみましょう。

✔ Part 7 に頻出の質問形式に慣れましょう。
- 文書のトピックや全体の内容を問う質問

    ex.　What is the purpose of the ～ ?　　What is the ～ about?
    　　　Why was the ～ sent?　　　　　　What does the ～ discuss?

Exercises for Part 7

次の通知文を読み、質問に答えましょう。

Dear Colleagues,

　It is my pleasure to announce the appointment of Dr. Thomas Adams to the position of R&D Director. He joins B & B Pharmaceuticals from Smith Pharmaceuticals, where he engaged in clinical product development planning.

　Throughout his career, Dr. Adams has made significant contributions in the area of Alzheimer's drugs, and some drugs he developed have already been used for the treatment of Alzheimer symptoms. He will be instrumental in expanding our clinical development efforts, and his appointment is a key step toward our goal of building a global clinical development capability.

　I'm sure he will be a valuable asset to our company.

---

1. What is this announcement about?
   (A) The development of drugs
   (B) The relocation of the company building
   (C) The introduction of a new employee
   (D) An appointment with a medical researcher
   Ⓐ Ⓑ Ⓒ Ⓓ

2. What is indicated about Dr. Adams?
   (A) He was a director at Smith Pharmaceuticals.
   (B) He will be responsible for clinical product development planning.
   (C) He developed some drugs, but it cost a large amount of money.
   (D) He has cured many Alzheimer patients.
   Ⓐ Ⓑ Ⓒ Ⓓ

MINI TOEIC L&R TEST

Listening Section

Part 1 Photographs 🔊 B-19

1.

Ⓐ Ⓑ Ⓒ Ⓓ

Part 2 Question-Response 🔊 B-20~22

2. Ⓐ Ⓑ Ⓒ
3. Ⓐ Ⓑ Ⓒ
4. Ⓐ Ⓑ Ⓒ

Part 3 Conversations 🔊 B-23~24

5. What position are the speakers thinking about for Joseph?
   (A) Assistant Designer
   (B) Consultant
   (C) Chief Director
   (D) Assistant Director
   Ⓐ Ⓑ Ⓒ Ⓓ

6. What is the man worried about?
   (A) The woman lost Joseph's résumé.
   (B) Joseph has the right qualifications.
   (C) Joseph isn't entirely suitable for the position.
   (D) Joseph doesn't have consultancy experience.
   Ⓐ Ⓑ Ⓒ Ⓓ

7. What are the speakers probably going to do next?
   (A) They'll talk to Joseph.
   (B) They'll call Joseph to double check.
   (C) They'll check Joseph's personal history.
   (D) They'll have another interview.
   Ⓐ Ⓑ Ⓒ Ⓓ

Unit 9 Employment

Part 4 Talks

🔊 B-25〜26

8. What does Highland Contracts do to avoid bothering customers?
   (A) Rent the company fleet
   (B) Replace tires
   (C) Arrange meetings
   (D) Visit Web sites
   Ⓐ Ⓑ Ⓒ Ⓓ

9. When do customers have access to the recovery service?
   (A) Only at night
   (B) The whole day
   (C) 24 days a month
   (D) Only in the day time
   Ⓐ Ⓑ Ⓒ Ⓓ

10. How can customers get more details about the company?
    (A) Calling a number
    (B) Visiting their Web site
    (C) Replacing a number
    (D) Offering a card
    Ⓐ Ⓑ Ⓒ Ⓓ

Reading Section

Part 5 Incomplete Sentences

11. The computer company intends to lay off as ------- 500 employees by April because of financial problems.
    (A) much as
    (B) more
    (C) many as
    (D) much more
    Ⓐ Ⓑ Ⓒ Ⓓ

12. The longer I stay in a stressful environment, ------- it is for my mental and physical health.
    (A) bad
    (B) badly
    (C) the worst
    (D) the worse
    Ⓐ Ⓑ Ⓒ Ⓓ

13. The Japanese clothing company earned its ------- profit in a decade in 2018.
    (A) large
    (B) larger
    (C) largest
    (D) more large
    Ⓐ Ⓑ Ⓒ Ⓓ

Part 6 Text Completion

Questions 14-16 refer to the following letter.

Dear Personnel Director:

This is in ------- to your classified advertisement for the position of copywriter in the March
14.
10 issue of *Jobweek* magazine. The position seems to fit very well with my education,
experience and interests. As my enclosed résumé indicates, I ------- at the headquarters
15.
of B & L Advertising in Los Angeles for the last five years as one of the chief copywriters.
Last year, I wrote an ad campaign for Panasony cell phone and it was its most profitable
one ever. -------. I am currently seeking other employment because I have decided to
16.
leave B & L Advertising to transfer to Detroit for personal reasons.

I look forward to meeting at your convenience to discuss your needs and my expertise more.

Sincerely,

Joe Fraser
Joe Fraser

14. (A) answer
    (B) response
    (C) resolution
    (D) request

15. (A) worked
    (B) have worked
    (C) had worked
    (D) am working

16. (A) I think I would make an excellent candidate for it.
    (B) Following is a sampling of the wide variety of projects I worked on.
    (C) Other projects include newspaper and radio ads for some clothing stores.
    (D) I have attached my résumé with this letter.

Unit 9 Employment 111

Part 7 Reading Comprehension

Questions 17-20 refer to the following announcement and e-mail.

Best Wishes!

Ms. Muller is retiring on June 1 after more than 25 years of devoted service at Metro Bank. We will miss her.

We are proud of Ms. Muller's work at Metro Bank. She began her career as a teller and eventually became the Director of Human Resources. Currently, she is leading a new program for employee development and training. We would like to celebrate her retirement and her contribution to the company. You are invited to attend the party to honor her.

The party, which includes dinner and dancing, will be held at Conference Hall on May 25 from 6 o'clock. We would like to take this opportunity to present Ms. Muller with a gift that will remind her of us for quite some time. On behalf of management, I would request each participant donate $10 towards the purchase of an appropriate gift.

Please notify Rebecca Hamilton by this Wednesday whether you will attend and who you will bring so we can prepare name tags.

To: Rebecca Hamilton
From: Robert Lee
Subject: Ms. Muller's retirement party

Thank you very much for your kind invitation to the retirement party for Ms. Muller.

She supervised me at the Bakersfield Branch for five years and has been a role model for novice employees, so I wouldn't miss the party for anything. My wife and daughter might be happy to be there and share her special day.

As for the gift, I suggest that we give her a china pot since she enjoys Chinese culture.

I look forward to meeting her again.

Best regards,
Robert

17. Which of the following statements is true about Ms. Muller?

(A) She has worked for more than 25 years as a teller.
(B) She is organizing a new customer service department.
(C) She was recently promoted to management.
(D) She is involved in employee education.

Ⓐ Ⓑ Ⓒ Ⓓ

18. What are attendees of the party required to do?

(A) Dance at the party
(B) Purchase a gift
(C) Bring some food
(D) Make contributions

Ⓐ Ⓑ Ⓒ Ⓓ

19. What is the main purpose of the e-mail?

(A) To confirm the place of an event
(B) To accept an invitation
(C) To provide details of a person's career
(D) To refuse an invitation

Ⓐ Ⓑ Ⓒ Ⓓ

20. What information does Mr. Lee still need to provide Ms. Hamilton with?

(A) His relationship with Ms. Muller
(B) The exact number of his party and their names
(C) The price of the gift
(D) A special food requirement

Ⓐ Ⓑ Ⓒ Ⓓ

| Listening Section | /10 | Reading Section | /10 | Total | /20 |

Unit 10
Lectures & Presentations

👍 Vocabulary Builder 🔊 B-27

A 語句の品詞と意味を書きましょう。

	品詞	意味		品詞	意味
1. presentation	( ) _____		6. optimize	( ) _____	
2. nervous	( ) _____		7. count on	( ) _____	
3. deadline	( ) _____		8. wrap up	( ) _____	
4. collaboration	( ) _____		9. focus on	( ) _____	
5. practical	( ) _____		10. set up	( ) _____	

B [ ]内の指示に従って単語を書き換えましょう。

1. nervous　　［名詞］⇨ _____　　3. collaboration ［動詞］⇨ _____
2. practical　　［動詞］⇨ _____　　4. set up　　　　［同義語］⇨ _____

114

Strategies for the Listening Section

🎧 Warm-Up Listening ◉ B-28

A アンとメグの会話を聞き、空所を埋めましょう。

Anne: Hey, Meg, it's your big day, isn't it? Shall I give you a ①_____ preparing for today's presentation?

Meg: Thanks, Anne. That's very kind ②_____ you. Would you make 20 ③_____ of the ④_____?

Anne: Sure, you can ⑤_____ on me.

Meg: I'm ⑥_____ nervous about the presentation. I wonder if they ⑦_____ like my project.

Anne: Go for it, Meg!

Meg: After working on that ⑧_____ for three months, I'm finally beginning to ⑨_____ things up. Please wish me ⑩_____.

B 登場人物の名前を自分の名前に置き換えて、パートナーと上の会話を練習しましょう。

💡 Tips for Part 2   意外な応答に慣れる

✔ Part 2 で出題される質問文は、疑問詞のWh-で始まる疑問文だけではなく、平叙文や付加疑問文、否定疑問文、orを使った二者択一文のこともあります。最後までよく聞いて、あらゆる疑問文に対応できるようにしましょう。

ex. **Q:** Aren't we sending each participant a map?
   A: There's one on the last page of the handout.

🎧 Let's Practice

次の各質問に合う応答をa～dから選びましょう。

1. Turn on the TV, will you?   (   )
2. How late did the meeting run?   (   )
3. Did you get through to anyone at the sales division?   (   )
4. You haven't been to England, have you?   (   )

> a. I called when the line wasn't busy.
> b. We finished up well past midnight.
> c. Of course, I have.
> d. But I want to concentrate on my homework.

Exercises for Part 2

A 質問に対する 3 つの応答を聞き、最も適切なものを選びましょう。　　🔊 B-29

1. Ⓐ Ⓑ Ⓒ
2. Ⓐ Ⓑ Ⓒ

B もう一度聞いて、質問の最初の 5 語を書き取りましょう。　　🔊 B-29

1. _____ _____ _____ _____ _____

2. _____ _____ _____ _____ _____

Strategies for the Reading Section

Warm-Up Reading B-30

A 英文を流れに沿って理解し、スピードを意識して速読しましょう。

We are happy to announce our collaboration with A & H Web Consulting to bring you the first E-commerce Online Store Workshop in Dallas. This workshop focuses not only on setting up the store but also helping you market your products. With this special collaboration, we are able to share with you practical tips on how you can have a great start for your online business. This workshop is a non-technical workshop aimed at business owners. The participants will learn 1) how to create their online store within 30 minutes, 2) how to configure their online store easily to suit their needs, 3) how to optimize their online store for Google so that their customers can find them. This workshop is made up of two evening sessions on 20 & 27 March. For further details about this workshop, please contact us by e-mail or call our toll free number.

(149 words) time [   ] wpm [   ]

B 上の英文の内容に関する質問に英語で答えましょう。

1. For whom is the announcement intended?
   _____

2. What can participants learn in the sessions?
   _____

3. How can people obtain more detailed information about the workshop?
   _____

Grammar Points | 仮定法

仮定法には、現在の事実と異なることを述べる仮定法過去、過去の事実と異なることを仮定する仮定法過去完了などがある。現実に起こり得ることについて表す場合は直説法を用いるのが一般的である。

　直説法：**If** it **rains** tomorrow, I **will give** you a lift to the station.（現実に起こり得ること）

　仮定法過去：**If** it **were** not rainy today, I **would go** for a drive.（現在の事実と異なること）

　仮定法過去完了：**If** Mark **had studied** hard, he **would have passed** the exam.
　　　　　　　　　　　　　　　　　　　　　　　　　　　（過去の事実と異なること）

注意すべき仮定法の表現
　I wish＋主語＋過去形：**I wish I could speak** English well.（現在の願望）
　I wish＋主語＋過去完了形（**had**＋過去分詞）：**I wish I had accepted** that job.
　　　　　　　　　　　　　　　　　　　　　　　　　　　（過去の事実と異なる願望）

Grammar Quiz （　）内の正しい語句を○で囲みましょう。

1. I wish I (had studied / studied) accounting when I was in college.
2. If you (didn't know / don't know) how to use the copier, ask any one of us.
3. I (could not have succeeded / cannot succeed) in my project, if it had not been for his encouragement.

Tips for Part 5　接頭辞と接尾辞をマスターして語彙を増やす

✔ 接頭辞は単語の頭について意味を変えますが、品詞自体は変わりません。接尾辞は語尾について品詞の種類を変え、中には意味が変わる語もあります。Part 5 の問題では、選択肢の単語の意味が明確にわからなくても、接尾辞から品詞を特定することが可能な場合も多くあります。

接頭辞：**in- / un-**（不、無）、**pre- / pro-**（前の）、**vice-**（副）、**co- / com- / con-**（ともに）
接尾辞：**-ation / -ment**（動詞→名詞）、**-al / -ic / -ous**（名詞→形容詞）、
　　　　-ate / -ize（形容詞→動詞）

Exercises for Part 5

文を完成させるのに、最も適切なものを選びましょう。

1. Our company's goal is to always make a ------- presentation of the product to the customer.
   (A) desire   (B) desirable   (C) desirably   (D) desirous

2. The speakers will explain how their research helps us understand ------- reality.
   (A) economy   (B) economical   (C) economics   (D) economic

3. Dr. Scott has ------- to deliver the keynote speech at the International Robot Fair.
   (A) coordinated   (B) conducted   (C) consented   (D) compared

4. The professor lectured that today's business students ------- need international perspectives.
   (A) urgently   (B) urgent   (C) urgency   (D) urge

5. The convention center designed by a celebrated architect was ------- in just a month.
   (A) construction   (B) constructed   (C) constructor   (D) constructional

MINI TOEIC L&R TEST

Listening Section

Part 1 Photographs ◉ B-31

1.

Ⓐ Ⓑ Ⓒ Ⓓ

Part 2 Question-Response ◉ B-32~34

2. Ⓐ Ⓑ Ⓒ
3. Ⓐ Ⓑ Ⓒ
4. Ⓐ Ⓑ Ⓒ

Part 3 Conversations ◉ B-35~36

5. How many factories does the woman's company have for each project?
   (A) 3
   (B) 13
   (C) 30
   (D) 33
   Ⓐ Ⓑ Ⓒ Ⓓ

6. How does the woman's company sell the products?
   (A) At the factory
   (B) In a certain country
   (C) Through exporting
   (D) Through retail outlets
   Ⓐ Ⓑ Ⓒ Ⓓ

7. What is the man planning to do?
   (A) Merge with the company
   (B) Invest in the company
   (C) Found a company
   (D) Take over the company
   Ⓐ Ⓑ Ⓒ Ⓓ

Part 4 Talks

8. What will be given on December 21?
   - (A) An anniversary ceremony
   - (B) An annual consultation
   - (C) A weekly lecture
   - (D) A yearly lecture

9. Where is the Borden Museum located?
   - (A) It is located on First Street.
   - (B) It is on the first floor of County Hall.
   - (C) It is next to Big Ben.
   - (D) It is opposite the London Eye.

10. What time will the lecture begin?
    - (A) 6:00 P.M.
    - (B) 6:30 P.M.
    - (C) 7:00 P.M.
    - (D) 8:00 P.M.

Reading Section

Part 5 Incomplete Sentences

11. If you had been late for the presentation, you ------- no chance of being promoted.
    - (A) would have had
    - (B) have
    - (C) will have
    - (D) had

12. Amy wishes she ------- her presentation in English during the international conference.
    - (A) could give
    - (B) were given
    - (C) will give
    - (D) can give

13. If the management ------- the defect of the new car model, they would not have introduced it at the motor show.
    - (A) realized
    - (B) had realized
    - (C) would realize
    - (D) would have realized

Part 6 Text Completion

Questions 14-16 refer to the following announcement.

Newcastle City Council will ------- Renewable Energy Spring Workshops at Silver
                                14.
Lake Visitor Center on April 10-12. These workshops are aimed to provide information to homeowners, businesses and governments on renewable energy options, such as biomass, solar, and geothermal. The opening event is scheduled for April 10 from 6:00 to 8:30. The session is titled "The Future Prospects of Renewable Energy" with a presentation from Dr. Kelly Richards of the GL Energy Institute. -------. In addition, two
                                                                              15.
workshops will be held to help homeowners and businesses ------- if solar works for their
                                                                      16.
home or business. Up to 40 places are available and there is a $15 fee for each of these workshops. For more information, please contact Brian Parker, the project manager for the workshops at 355-4681.

14. (A) hosts
    (B) hosting
    (C) be hosting
    (D) be hosted
    Ⓐ Ⓑ Ⓒ Ⓓ

15. (A) This event is free for Newcastle residents.
    (B) Our city has a range of renewable energy systems throughout our Newcastle facilities.
    (C) The participants will learn how to analyze the cost effectiveness of solar installation.
    (D) The international conference on renewable energy will be held on May 24.
    Ⓐ Ⓑ Ⓒ Ⓓ

16. (A) determination
    (B) determine
    (C) determinant
    (D) determined
    Ⓐ Ⓑ Ⓒ Ⓓ

Part 7 Reading Comprehension

Questions 17-18 refer to the following notice.

> TO: All office employees
> FROM: Jeff Porter
> SUBJECT: Informative presentation
>
> TechGlobal, the Internet provider in NY, is offering an informative presentation on their new Internet conferencing technologies.
>
> Virtual meetings can save money and protect the environment by eliminating travel. Online presentations and meetings have now become the norm, and many organizations make use of some form of virtual meeting on the Internet.
>
> You will learn how the WEBCON software can support videoconferencing on the Internet and learn about teleconferencing tools, including whiteboards and Web tours. The presentation will take place on Tuesday June 20, 10:30 A.M. in Room #301.
>
> All employees are invited to attend. This will be a great opportunity for all of us to see and experience cutting edge Internet communication tools. Please notify Bob in the R & D section by June 16, if you will be attending.

17. What is the main subject of the notice?
    (A) Reduction of travel expenses
    (B) Opportunities of employee education
    (C) Organizations that use Internet conferencing
    (D) Development of new computer software

18. What will be discussed at the presentation?
    (A) How to help the environment by getting rid of travel
    (B) How to use teleconferencing software and tools
    (C) How to save money by conducting virtual meetings
    (D) How to sell Internet communication tools

Questions 19-20 refer to the following information.

Green Economics Lecture Series

UH is organizing an exciting lecture series on green economics to be held on three Fridays at 4:00 P.M. throughout this fall.

- Join us Friday, September 20th from 4:00–5:15 P.M. at Davidson Hall 003 for the first lecture featuring professor of sociology at Brown College, Elana Friedman! Her most recent book is *The Economics of True Wealth*.

- October 11th will feature Northeastern University's economics professor and author of *Rethinking Globalization*, John Adams. (4:00–5:15 in Bakery Hall 003)

- On November 1st our speaker will be UH's own public affairs professor Eric Lopez, an expert in urban and regional economics, and transportation planning and environmental policy. (4:00–5:15 in Bakery Hall 002)

If you are planning to attend these lectures, please refer to www2.Coming_to_an_event at UH.htm or contact Tracy Hiner at (918)-234-5186.

19. Who wrote the book *Rethinking Globalization*?
    (A) Elana Friedman
    (B) Eric Lopez
    (C) John Adams
    (D) Tracy Hiner

20. Where will the lecture by Eric Lopez be held?
    (A) At Bakery Hall 002
    (B) At Bakery Hall 003
    (C) At Davidson Hall 002
    (D) At Davidson Hall 003

Listening Section ___/10   Reading Section ___/10   Total ___/20

Unit 11
Business Affairs (1)

Vocabulary Builder ◉ B-39

A 語句の品詞と意味を書きましょう。

	品詞	意味		品詞	意味
1. guarantee	( )	_____	6. profitability	( )	_____
2. compliment	( )	_____	7. acquisition	( )	_____
3. term	( )	_____	8. reinforce	( )	_____
4. competition	( )	_____	9. enlarge	( )	_____
5. e-tailer	( )	_____	10. compromise	( )	_____

B [ ]内の指示に従って単語を書き換えましょう。

1. competition　［動詞］⇨ _____
2. profitability　［形容詞］⇨ _____
3. acquisition　［動詞］⇨ _____
4. reinforce　［名詞］⇨ _____

Strategies for the Listening Section

🎧 Warm-Up Listening   ⏵B-40

A ピーターとタカシの電話での会話を聞き、空所を埋めましょう。

Peter: Hello, Takashi. I have good news for you.
Takashi: I can't wait to hear ①_____, Peter.
Peter: We're ready to sign your ②_____.
Takashi: Great! Trust me, I can ③_____ that you made the right decision.
Peter: I like the ④_____ you have for your work. This ⑤_____ is only possible because of your ⑥_____. You should be proud of ⑦_____.
Takashi: Thank you for the ⑧_____. I hope we'll have a ⑨_____ business relationship.
Peter: I'd like you to come to our office when it's convenient for you, Takashi.
Takashi: Sure ⑩_____.

B 登場人物の名前を自分の名前に置き換えて、パートナーと上の会話を練習しましょう。

💡 Tips for Part 3   選択肢から会話の内容を予想する

✔ 会話が流れる前に質問文と選択肢に目を通して、会話の内容を予想します。音声を聞きながら会話をしている人の職業、会話が行われている場所や状況などを推測して正答を判断します。

🗨 Let's Practice

次の2つの質問と選択肢を読んで予想できる会話の内容を推測し、「① 誰が　② どこで　③ 何を　④ いつ」にあてはまる日本語を入れましょう。

1. When is the man going to take the management course at college?
   (A) In April   (B) In July   (C) In September   (D) In January

2. Why is the man going to attend the orientation this Saturday?
   (A) To get a ticket
   (B) To get some advice from his counselor
   (C) To fill in a job application form
   (D) To find some friends

1. ①_____ が ②_____ で経営学のコースを受講しようとしている。
2. 何らかの目的のために、コースを受講する前に ③_____ を ④_____ に受けることに決めた。

Unit 11 Business Affairs (1)

Exercises for Part 3

A 会話を聞いて、質問に対する正しい答えを選びましょう。　　　　　　　　　　B-41

1. What does the man do?
   (A) He writes for the press.
   (B) He works for a library.
   (C) He owns a discount store.
   (D) He works for an e-tailer.

   Ⓐ Ⓑ Ⓒ Ⓓ

2. Where is the conversation most likely taking place?
   (A) In a taxi
   (B) At a reception desk
   (C) In a conference room
   (D) On the Internet

   Ⓐ Ⓑ Ⓒ Ⓓ

3. What does the woman mean when she says, "this is incredible"?
   (A) She thinks what the man says is a terrible lie.
   (B) She thinks what the man says is amazingly good.
   (C) She doesn't trust e-commerce.
   (D) She doesn't think she can make it.

   Ⓐ Ⓑ Ⓒ Ⓓ

Strategies for the Reading Section

📖 Warm-Up Reading 🔊 B-42

A 英文を流れに沿って理解し、スピードを意識して速読しましょう。

Today, Max Healthcare Inc., a leading health care company, has placed a $3.25 billion takeover bid on another health care company, H.L.Care Group Inc. The acquisition is expected to reinforce Max's position as a leading integrated health care provider and place it among the top 100 listed companies based on market capitalization. The deal is further expected to enlarge and improve Max's service offerings and geographic coverage, and generate anticipated synergies and operational improvements of $80 million to $95 million in fiscal year 2020.

"Max's acquisition of H.L.Care Group is undoubtedly the start of an exciting new phase in the development of our company," said Mark Brown, co-founder of H.L.Care Group Inc. "The addition of H.L.Care's services to Max's offerings will provide greater access to important screening facilities for a larger number of patients."

(134 words)　time _____　wpm _____

B 上の英文の内容に関する質問に英語で答えましょう。

1. What happened between Max Healthcare, Inc. and H.L.Care Group Inc. today?
   _____

2. How will Max Healthcare Inc. benefit from the event?
   _____

3. Who is Mark Brown?
   _____

Grammar Points　関係詞

関係代名詞は接続詞と代名詞の働きを持ち、関係副詞は接続詞と副詞の働きを持つ。

ex. I want a skilled man **who** will help us in our project.（主格）
The man **whose** house you looked at will move overseas.（所有格）
The man to **whom** you talked on the phone is the sales manager.（目的格）
The bookstore **where** I bought the book is just around the corner.（関係副詞）
I've forgotten the year **when** our company was founded.（関係副詞）

Grammar Quiz　（　）内の正しい語を○で囲みましょう。

1. The man (who / whom) sent me a copy of the book is my former colleague.
2. The library (which / where) I study has a unique collection of books.
3. (Whenever / However) you sign a contract, you should go over the details.

Tips for Part 7 — ダブルパッセージの問題に慣れる

✔ Part 7で出題される2つで1セットの長文（ダブルパッセージ）には、Eメールやビジネスレターのやりとり、求人広告と応募の手紙、注文とそれに対する返信など、さまざまなパターンがあります。パッセージがどんな種類のものか、誰が誰に対して書いているのかなどに注意しましょう。

Exercises for Part 7

次の2つの手紙を読み、質問に答えましょう。

Dear Mr. Everson:

Thank you for your price quotation (your ref. No. 752) of July 1. We have examined your price carefully and would like to ask if an additional 10 percent reduction is possible. If you could compromise on the price for this order, we will increase our order. If you accept this condition, then we will order 800 units of the HX-05 shopping cart instead of 500.

I would appreciate a reply by July 15.

Sincerely,
Jeremy Norton

Dear Mr. Norton:

Thank you for your letter. We have concluded that we can reduce the price by 20 percent, which is 5 percent more than our previous offer. We are sorry that we are unable to fully comply with your request.

Please review the attached draft of our contract and let us know of any comments or questions you may have. We look forward to receiving your order confirmation.

Sincerely,
Greg Everson

---

1. What is Mr. Norton requesting?
   (A) Another order
   (B) The reduction of the number of units
   (C) A change in the payment method
   (D) An additional discount
   Ⓐ Ⓑ Ⓒ Ⓓ

2. When did Mr. Norton expect to receive Mr. Everson's reply?
   (A) By July 1
   (B) By July 10
   (C) By July 15
   (D) By July 20
   Ⓐ Ⓑ Ⓒ Ⓓ

3. What kind of information is mentioned in Mr. Everson's letter?
   (A) Questions on the contract
   (B) A partial acceptance of Mr. Norton's request
   (C) The details of the final draft
   (D) The reference number
   Ⓐ Ⓑ Ⓒ Ⓓ

MINI TOEIC L&R TEST

Listening Section

Part 1 Photographs   ◁)) B-43

1.

Ⓐ Ⓑ Ⓒ Ⓓ

Part 2 Question-Response   ◁)) B-44~46

2. Ⓐ Ⓑ Ⓒ
3. Ⓐ Ⓑ Ⓒ
4. Ⓐ Ⓑ Ⓒ

Part 3 Conversations   ◁)) B-47~48

5. What is the conversation mainly about?

   (A) A video game
   (B) A VR device
   (C) Medical training
   (D) A warranty period

   Ⓐ Ⓑ Ⓒ Ⓓ

6. What will the woman probably do next?

   (A) Put on goggles
   (B) Try on a dress
   (C) Work in the office
   (D) Purchase a VR device

   Ⓐ Ⓑ Ⓒ Ⓓ

7. What does the woman mean when she says, "Just a second"?

   (A) She is eager to buy the product.
   (B) She finds the device too difficult to use.
   (C) She is sure the device is worthy of praise.
   (D) She is hesitating to purchase the device.

   Ⓐ Ⓑ Ⓒ Ⓓ

Unit 11 Business Affairs (1)   129

Part 4 Talks

🔊 B-49~50

8. What is being advertised?
   - (A) A car
   - (B) A washing machine
   - (C) A dishwasher
   - (D) A vacuum cleaner

   Ⓐ Ⓑ Ⓒ Ⓓ

9. When was it produced?
   - (A) In 2015
   - (B) In 2016
   - (C) In 2017
   - (D) In 2018

   Ⓐ Ⓑ Ⓒ Ⓓ

10. How can listeners get more information?
    - (A) By visiting the office
    - (B) By visiting the Web site
    - (C) By calling or e-mailing
    - (D) By sending a letter

    Ⓐ Ⓑ Ⓒ Ⓓ

Reading Section

Part 5 Incomplete Sentences

11. There are certain circumstances ------- you may withdraw from the contract.
    - (A) whom
    - (B) where
    - (C) that
    - (D) which

    Ⓐ Ⓑ Ⓒ Ⓓ

12. The electronics corporation has apologized to each customer ------- order was delayed.
    - (A) who
    - (B) whose
    - (C) whom
    - (D) that

    Ⓐ Ⓑ Ⓒ Ⓓ

13. Parties ------- enter into contracts can rely on the contracts to structure their business relationships.
    - (A) whose
    - (B) how
    - (C) whom
    - (D) who

    Ⓐ Ⓑ Ⓒ Ⓓ

Part 6 Text Completion

Questions 14-16 refer to the following advertisement.

Leading Worldwide LED Company

NCC LEDlight Tec was established in March 2005. Our company has grown to be one of the leading LED screen display companies in the US. NCC LEDlight Tec is a manufacturer of LED video screens and billboards, electronic signs and displays and more, for advertising, stadiums and live events. We understand the importance of ------- **14.** communication.

-------. **15.** So if you are looking to make a move and you are a highly motivated professional ------- **16.** welcomes new challenges, please take a look at www.nccledlight.cc. We have your next great opportunity! Work with NCC LEDlight Tec in your country as our agent and earn a lot of money from commission by connecting us to potential buyers or outdoor advertising companies.

---

14. (A) verbal
    (B) audible
    (C) visual
    (D) touchy

15. (A) We are attaching some Information about NCC LEDlight Tec.
    (B) We are now seeking highly skilled professionals to take us even further.
    (C) Our headquarters is located in Pittsburgh, Pennsylvania.
    (D) In addition to providing screens, we support customers who have their own screens.

16. (A) who
    (B) what
    (C) whom
    (D) which

Part 7   Reading Comprehension

Questions 17-20 refer to the following advertisement and agreement.

Sunshine Baby Rentals

Serving San Francisco, Bay Area,
Los Angeles and Orange County
2531 E Burbank Blvd #107
Burbank, CA 81405
Phone: 818-350-3621
Web site: www.sunshinebabyrentals.com

We provide a large inventory of baby equipment, stroller rental and other necessities for families traveling with children in the Northern and Southern California area. Whether you are going to Disneyland or traveling across the Golden Gate Bridge, we strive to make your trip trouble-free.

All of our inventory is purchased new and has the original manufacturer stickers on them. All of our equipment is completely safe, checked and sanitized.

◇ Rent 2 or more items below and get 15% off.
  • Full Crib • Baby Monitor • Car Seat • Single Stroller • Umbrella Stroller
◇ Rent more than 7 days and get 20% off.
◇ No charge for the end date if items are returned for driver to pick up by 10 A.M.
◇ Later evening and early morning delivery available without additional charge.

Rental Agreement

CUSTOMER NAME: _Jill Douglas_   CUSTOMER PHONE: _917-237-5077_
DELIVERY DATE: _March 7_   TIME: _7:00 A.M._   PICK UP DATE: _March 17_   TIME: _9:00 A.M._
RENTAL ITEMS: _1 car seat, 1 tricycle for toddler_

The undersigned renter agrees that the rented items will at all times remain the property of the rental agent, Sunshine Baby Rentals ("SBR"). There will be an additional charge for rental items returned with parts missing or in exceptionally dirty condition. If the item(s) are returned damaged, the renter will be obligated to pay the accumulated rental fee plus the cost of repair. If the item(s) are in irreparable condition, the renter shall be obligated to purchase the item(s) at the suggested retail price. This does not apply to ordinary wear and tear.

The exact length of time items are to be rented will be written on the contract. The length of the rental agreement may be changed only by a phone call and verbal permission prior to the original written return date. It is the responsibility of the renter to contact SBR about any changes.

The undersigned has read and agrees to the above contract.

SIGNED: _Jill Douglas_   DATE: _March 1_

17. Who would most likely be attracted to this advertisement?
    (A) Families that live in the Northern California
    (B) Families that are going to travel in Western California
    (C) Families that are leaving Los Angeles for New York
    (D) Families that are going to take a trip to Orange County
    Ⓐ Ⓑ Ⓒ Ⓓ

18. What is true about Ms. Douglas's rental terms?
    (A) She will receive a 15% discount.
    (B) She won't pay for the last day.
    (C) She has to return the rental items to the store.
    (D) She will be required to pay an additional delivery fee.
    Ⓐ Ⓑ Ⓒ Ⓓ

19. What should customers do if an item is returned in irreparable condition?
    (A) Pay the accumulated rental fee plus the cost of repair
    (B) Purchase a new one and replace it
    (C) Buy the item at the suggested retail price
    (D) Visit a nearby repair shop
    Ⓐ Ⓑ Ⓒ Ⓓ

20. Why is it necessary for customers to sign their names?
    (A) To charge items on their credit card
    (B) To buy insurance against damage
    (C) To agree to the contract
    (D) To purchase baby goods
    Ⓐ Ⓑ Ⓒ Ⓓ

Listening Section /10 **Reading Section** /10 **Total** /20

Unit 12
Business Affairs (2)

👍 Vocabulary Builder 🔊 B-51

A 語句の品詞と意味を書きましょう。

	品詞	意味		品詞	意味
1. convince	( )	_____	6. promotion	( )	_____
2. boom	( )	_____	7. budget	( )	_____
3. extension	( )	_____	8. ensure	( )	_____
4. bankruptcy	( )	_____	9. venue	( )	_____
5. brochure	( )	_____	10. supplier	( )	_____

B [ ]内の指示に従って単語を書き換えましょう。

1. extension　［動詞］⇨ _____　　3. bankruptcy　［形容詞］⇨ _____
2. promotion　［動詞］⇨ _____　　4. supplier　［動詞］⇨ _____

Strategies for the Listening Section

🎧 Warm-Up Listening 🔊 B-52

A ウィルとジョンの会話を聞き、空所を埋めましょう。

Will: I ①_____ your taking time to meet with me, John. But I'm ②_____ that I won't waste your time. I understand your business is ③_____ here.

John: So ④_____ so good. We've made constant ⑤_____. But competition ⑥_____ harder and harder.

Will: That's ⑦_____ I can help you. Have you seen the ⑧_____ for our new video games?

John: Yes. We're very interested in the new ⑨_____, Will.

Will: I'm glad you like it. We can set up a demonstration ⑩_____.

B 登場人物の名前を自分の名前に置き換えて、パートナーと上の会話を練習しましょう。

💡 Tips for Part 4　頻出ジャンルの質問パターンに慣れる

✔ Part 4で出題される説明文のジャンルは、公共の場でのアナウンス、コマーシャル、ニュース、天気予報、会議や講演の前のスピーチなど多岐にわたります。不特定多数を対象とする説明文の場合、出題される質問パターンに慣れてしまえば、すばやく正答を見つけることができます。

🗣 Let's Practice

太字のキーワードだけを見て質問文の意味を推測し、パートナーと確認しましょう。

> **ex. What** is the **announcement about**?
> ⇨「何についてのアナウンス?」

1. **What** is the **topic** of the **speech**?
   ⇨ _____

2. **Who** most likely is the **speaker**?
   ⇨ _____

3. According to the advertisement, **who** would be most **interested in** 〜?
   ⇨ _____

Unit 12 Business Affairs (2)

Exercises for Part 4

A 先に質問文の太字部分だけを読み、その後で説明文を聞いて、正しい答えを選びましょう。　🔊 B-53

1. **What** is the **topic** of the **news item**?
   - (A) Profitability
   - (B) Extension of an agreement
   - (C) Expiration of contract
   - (D) Mobile phones

   Ⓐ Ⓑ Ⓒ Ⓓ

2. **When** was the **deadline** for the **contracts** between the union and Star?
   - (A) November 12
   - (B) November 20
   - (C) December 12
   - (D) December 20

   Ⓐ Ⓑ Ⓒ Ⓓ

B 説明文をもう一度聞いて、（　）に適語を入れましょう。　🔊 B-53

The Workers Union and Star Mobile Phone agreed to (① 　　　　　) their contracts. The contracts between the union and Star were (② 　　　　　) to expire at 12:00 P.M. on November (③ 　　　　　). The union granted Star an (④ 　　　　　) in advance of the deadline, as it concentrated on reaching a deal with Star. The union is (⑤ 　　　　　) to seek a slightly better contract agreement from Star Mobile. We hope everything will go well.

Strategies for the Reading Section

📖 Warm-Up Reading　　　🔊 B-54

A 英文を流れに沿って理解し、スピードを意識して速読しましょう。

Various types of advertisements are used to increase sales of products or services in today's corporate world. Although TV is the most popular advertising media in the U.S., the Internet is rapidly becoming an important advertising venue. If you have a limited budget, one advantage of Internet advertising is that it can be much more in reach than traditional methods, such as newspaper and TV advertising. Another advantage is that it opens new possibilities to spread messages to a specific target audience. Internet advertising offers some targeting methods that ensure that the audiences who see your ads are the ones most likely to buy. In addition, by using the World Wide Web, you reach people all over the world, not just in your country. Businesses will profit from the use of Internet advertising because it is cheaper and more effective when compared to traditional media.

(145 words)　time [　　　]　wpm [　　　]

B 上の英文の内容に関する質問に英語で答えましょう。

1. What does the article discuss?
   _____

2. What are the traditional ways of advertising?
   _____

3. What benefits can Internet advertisers expect?
   _____

Grammar Points　｜　接続詞

等位接続詞：and、but、or、so、for、nor など。
- **ex.** I had to complete many tasks using my computer **but** it was running so slow.

従属接続詞：when、while、although、because、if、whether など。
- **ex.** Shelly fell asleep on the job **because** she was up all night working on the project.

注意すべき接続詞：
- **even if ...**「たとえ…でも」
  - **ex.** **Even if** you are wrong, you should not admit it.
- **both A and B**「AもBも両方」
  - **ex.** Our company has branches in **both** Tokyo **and** Paris.

Grammar Quiz　（　）内の正しい語を○で囲みましょう。

1. (Although / When) we installed a new machine to increase efficiency, we haven't made much profit yet.
2. (Unless / If) I receive my visa by tomorrow, I have to put off my departure.
3. The sales clerk says she can't afford to live on her salary (because / so) she's going to start looking for another job.

Tips for Part 7　記入用紙の書式に慣れる

✔ アンケート用紙や雑誌の購読申込用紙など、どのような情報を記入するのかということを把握しておきましょう。また、タイトルや見出しを拾い読みして内容を推測してみましょう。

Exercises for Part 7

次の申し込み用紙を読み、質問に答えましょう。

World Home Expo Australia July 15–17

WHEA is the foremost consumer product show in Australia, presenting a wide selection of houseware, kitchenware, tableware, bathroom accessories as well as home décor items. It will prove to be the sourcing destination for all importers, wholesalers, distributors, retail chains and specialty stores for a variety of houseware products.

Registration Form for Foreign Visitors

Name _____　Title _____
Age _____
Company _____　Address _____
Country _____　Business Phone _____
Mobile Phone _____　E-mail _____
Number of people attending _____

Products Interested in:

☐ House Décor Products　　☐ Tableware
☐ Bar Accessories　　　　　☐ Household Products
☐ Kitchenware　　　　　　　☐ Lighting
☐ Home Utilities & Accessories　☐ Hotel Ware

[Submit]

---

1. Who is the event aimed at?
   (A) Real estate agencies
   (B) Furniture and home accessory stores
   (C) Food importers
   (D) Wholesalers of office supplies
   Ⓐ Ⓑ Ⓒ Ⓓ

2. What information is necessary to register for the event?
   (A) A person's fax number
   (B) A person's birthdate
   (C) A person's gender
   (D) A person's status
   Ⓐ Ⓑ Ⓒ Ⓓ

MINI TOEIC L&R TEST

Listening Section

Part 1 Photographs 🔊 B-55

1.

Ⓐ Ⓑ Ⓒ Ⓓ

Part 2 Question-Response 🔊 B-56~58

2. Ⓐ Ⓑ Ⓒ
3. Ⓐ Ⓑ Ⓒ
4. Ⓐ Ⓑ Ⓒ

Part 3 Conversations 🔊 B-59~60

5. Which region of Japan are the speakers talking about?
   (A) Northwest
   (B) West
   (C) Southeast
   (D) East
   Ⓐ Ⓑ Ⓒ Ⓓ

6. What does the woman say about the target?
   (A) It is 5,400 units.
   (B) It hasn't been met.
   (C) It is a big problem.
   (D) It needs to be changed.
   Ⓐ Ⓑ Ⓒ Ⓓ

7. What do the speakers think is needed as a solution?
   (A) Some assets
   (B) They don't know yet.
   (C) Some property
   (D) It is a secret.
   Ⓐ Ⓑ Ⓒ Ⓓ

Unit 12 Business Affairs (2) 139

Part 4 Talks 🔊 B-61~62

JAVA-1	$720	*installed with a variety of functions
TURBO-2	$550	*10% OFF when you buy two
DUSTER I	$540	*powerful enough to clean three rooms
C-BOY	$458	*square shape

8. What is being advertised?
   (A) Cars
   (B) Sensors
   (C) Vacuum cleaners
   (D) Washing machines
   Ⓐ Ⓑ Ⓒ Ⓓ

9. Which function is JAVA-1 installed with?
   (A) An infrared sensor
   (B) An area memory function
   (C) A fall prevention sensor
   (D) An ultrasonic sensor
   Ⓐ Ⓑ Ⓒ Ⓓ

10. Look at the graphic. How much is a vacuum cleaner with a triangular shape?
    (A) $458
    (B) $540
    (C) $550
    (D) $720
    Ⓐ Ⓑ Ⓒ Ⓓ

Reading Section

Part 5 Incomplete Sentences

11. ------- the cost of advertising is quite high, the benefits in the long run balance the high cost.
    (A) So
    (B) Because
    (C) Although
    (D) Before
    Ⓐ Ⓑ Ⓒ Ⓓ

12. The Chinese food and beverage market is becoming increasingly sophisticated by supplying ------- local and imported products.
    (A) so
    (B) both
    (C) and
    (D) either
    Ⓐ Ⓑ Ⓒ Ⓓ

13. Many shoppers use coupons ------- they shop for grocery and household items at supermarkets.
    (A) when
    (B) because
    (C) although
    (D) unless
    Ⓐ Ⓑ Ⓒ Ⓓ

Part 6 Text Completion

Questions 14-16 refer to the following advertisement.

What can Smart Creative Marketing do for you?

Smart Creative Marketing is a Seattle based marketing firm that offers award-winning creative services, powerful Internet marketing, quality printing, and exceptional photo & video production. We use the best ------- who will capture incredible images, enhancing our designs.
                                            14.

Do you need better results from your marketing?

You may have a wonderful product or service, but ------- your marketing is exceptionally good, your business will fail to achieve its full potential. -------. With years of experience promoting businesses and brands in fresh and effective ways, we are able to offer full marketing support.
                                                            15.   **16.**

---

14. (A) mechanics
    (B) composers
    (C) photographers
    (D) operators

    Ⓐ Ⓑ Ⓒ Ⓓ

15. (A) unless
    (B) when
    (C) while
    (D) because

    Ⓐ Ⓑ Ⓒ Ⓓ

16. (A) The clients we work with fall into four main groups.
    (B) Choosing the best partner to help you reach your goals is crucial.
    (C) Initial meetings are free of charge.
    (D) We work in many other industry sectors.

    Ⓐ Ⓑ Ⓒ Ⓓ

Part 7 Reading Comprehension

Questions 17-20 refer to the following advertisement, form, and customer review.

AirPerfect Co.

We offer the most affordable, truly comprehensive air purifier ever. Now is the time to upgrade beyond basic allergen removal and advance to actual health protection. Join our thousands of satisfied customers and make an investment in a healthier, longer life!

Before you buy other manufacturers' air purifiers, compare the AirPerfect AZ-7 for yourself. The AirPerfect air purifier offers more technology and cleans your air nearly three times as fast.

We'd be delighted to offer a risk-free 60-day trial. If you are not completely satisfied, return the AirPerfect air purifier for a full refund. We will even pay return shipping costs, so there is no risk to you. To find out more, give us a call or check off the appropriate box on the enclosed reply card and mail it today.

AirPerfect Co.

Thank you for your interest in our products and services. Please complete this form and send it to us. We will get back to you as soon as possible.

Name: Kevin Olson   *Phone:* (578) 355-8244
Address: 201 S. Wilmot Rd., Nashville TN, 35721
E-mail: kolsonma@cmail.com

1. Please check the information package you would like to receive:
   [✓] Product Information   [✓] Price Information   [ ] Company Information
2. How would you like to receive this information?
   [ ] By E-mail   [✓] By Regular Mail   [ ] By Fax   [ ] Call me
3. Have you ever heard of air purifiers?   [✓] Yes   [ ] No
4. If yes, what do you think an air purifier does?
   [ ] Filters smoke, fumes, toxic gases   [✓] Filters dust particles, mites, pet dander
   [ ] Filters chemicals and solvents   [ ] Filters bacteria, viruses, fungi and molds
   [✓] Removes bad odors   [✓] Delivers clean air
   [ ] All of the above
5. Do you have an air purifier at your organization/ home?   [✓] Yes   [ ] No
6. If yes, which brand of air purifier do you have?   Green Air 1000
7. Additional requests or comments: I am allergic to pollen and dust and I bought an air purifier several years ago. It seems like the odor eliminating function isn't working efficiently anymore, so I'm thinking of replacing it.

Customer Review

Product Reviews for AirPerfect AZ-7
August 26
Kevin Olson

★★★★★ Excellent Product

I've had the AirPerfect AZ-7 for a few weeks. I feel it has helped ease my hay fever and dust allergies. Although I have had an irritating cough at night and itching eyes for years, I have a good night's sleep with a clear nose now. Also, my room doesn't smell at all.

This device is suitable for the size of the bedroom and completely silent. I thoroughly recommend this product.

17. According to the advertisement, what feature of the AirPerfect product is superior to the other companies' products?

(A) Its design
(B) Its color
(C) Its energy efficiency
(D) Its speed

Ⓐ Ⓑ Ⓒ Ⓓ

18. What is emphasized about services provided by AirPerfect Co.?

(A) It has a money-back guarantee.
(B) It delivers the product within a few days.
(C) It provides 60-day free repair.
(D) It offers online customer support.

Ⓐ Ⓑ Ⓒ Ⓓ

19. What information does Mr. Olson NOT need to provide?

(A) What information package he wants
(B) Whether he has an air purifier or not
(C) How much he can spend on a new product
(D) What knowledge he has about air purifiers

Ⓐ Ⓑ Ⓒ Ⓓ

20. What feature of AirPerfect AZ-7 does Mr. Olson think is better than his previous air purifier?

(A) The energy-saving system
(B) The deodorization device
(C) The size
(D) The noise

Ⓐ Ⓑ Ⓒ Ⓓ

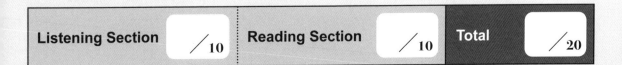

Listening Section ___/10   Reading Section ___/10   Total ___/20

MINI TOEIC L&R TEST スコア記録表

Unit	Listening Section	Reading Section	Total Points	% (Total / 20 x 100)	wpm
1					
2					
3					
4					
5					
6					
7					
8					
9					
10					
11					
12					
AVERAGE	/ 10	/ 10	/ 20	%	

自己分析表 [記入例]

	Unit & Topic	評価できる点	改善すべき点
Best Listening	U.2 Entertainment	Part 1 & 2 は全部正解した。	Part 4 の問題をできるだけ先に読んでおく。
Best Reading	U.3 Travel	Part 7 は全部正解した。	Part 5 の文法をもっと強化する。
Worst Listening	U.11 Business (1)	Part 1 は OK！	Part 4 のビジネス系の単語の聞き取りの訓練。
Worst Reading	U.12 Business (2)	Part 5 は OK！	Part 6 のビジネス単語力が弱い！

MINI TOEIC L&R TEST 記録グラフ

Student ID _____

NAME _____

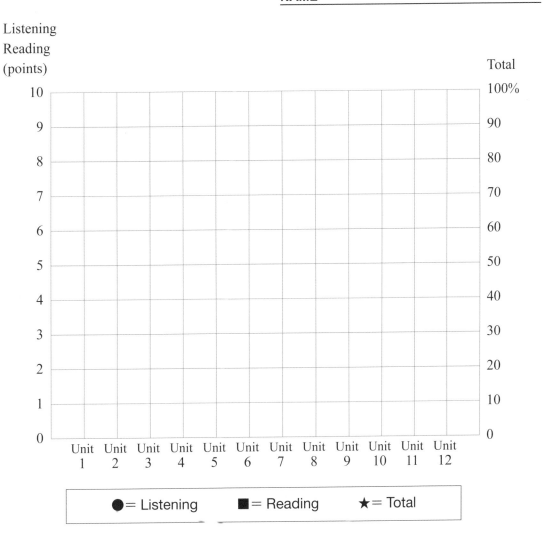

自己分析表 〈記入例は p.144 にあります。〉

	Unit & Topic	評価できる点	改善すべき点
Best Listening			
Best Reading			
Worst Listening			
Worst Reading			

Pre-test 解答用紙

Student ID	
フリガナ	
NAME 氏　名	

LISTENING SECTION

Part 1		Part 2		Part 3		Part 4	
No.	ANSWER A B C D	No.	ANSWER A B C	No.	ANSWER A B C D	No.	ANSWER A B C D
1	Ⓐ Ⓑ Ⓒ Ⓓ	3	Ⓐ Ⓑ Ⓒ	11	Ⓐ Ⓑ Ⓒ Ⓓ	20	Ⓐ Ⓑ Ⓒ Ⓓ
2	Ⓐ Ⓑ Ⓒ Ⓓ	4	Ⓐ Ⓑ Ⓒ	12	Ⓐ Ⓑ Ⓒ Ⓓ	21	Ⓐ Ⓑ Ⓒ Ⓓ
		5	Ⓐ Ⓑ Ⓒ	13	Ⓐ Ⓑ Ⓒ Ⓓ	22	Ⓐ Ⓑ Ⓒ Ⓓ
		6	Ⓐ Ⓑ Ⓒ	14	Ⓐ Ⓑ Ⓒ Ⓓ	23	Ⓐ Ⓑ Ⓒ Ⓓ
		7	Ⓐ Ⓑ Ⓒ	15	Ⓐ Ⓑ Ⓒ Ⓓ	24	Ⓐ Ⓑ Ⓒ Ⓓ
		8	Ⓐ Ⓑ Ⓒ	16	Ⓐ Ⓑ Ⓒ Ⓓ	25	Ⓐ Ⓑ Ⓒ Ⓓ
		9	Ⓐ Ⓑ Ⓒ	17	Ⓐ Ⓑ Ⓒ Ⓓ		
		10	Ⓐ Ⓑ Ⓒ	18	Ⓐ Ⓑ Ⓒ Ⓓ		
				19	Ⓐ Ⓑ Ⓒ Ⓓ		

READING SECTION

Part 5		Part 6		Part 7	
No.	ANSWER A B C D	No.	ANSWER A B C D	No.	ANSWER A B C D
26	Ⓐ Ⓑ Ⓒ Ⓓ	36	Ⓐ Ⓑ Ⓒ Ⓓ	40	Ⓐ Ⓑ Ⓒ Ⓓ
27	Ⓐ Ⓑ Ⓒ Ⓓ	37	Ⓐ Ⓑ Ⓒ Ⓓ	41	Ⓐ Ⓑ Ⓒ Ⓓ
28	Ⓐ Ⓑ Ⓒ Ⓓ	38	Ⓐ Ⓑ Ⓒ Ⓓ	42	Ⓐ Ⓑ Ⓒ Ⓓ
29	Ⓐ Ⓑ Ⓒ Ⓓ	39	Ⓐ Ⓑ Ⓒ Ⓓ	43	Ⓐ Ⓑ Ⓒ Ⓓ
30	Ⓐ Ⓑ Ⓒ Ⓓ			44	Ⓐ Ⓑ Ⓒ Ⓓ
31	Ⓐ Ⓑ Ⓒ Ⓓ			45	Ⓐ Ⓑ Ⓒ Ⓓ
32	Ⓐ Ⓑ Ⓒ Ⓓ			46	Ⓐ Ⓑ Ⓒ Ⓓ
33	Ⓐ Ⓑ Ⓒ Ⓓ			47	Ⓐ Ⓑ Ⓒ Ⓓ
34	Ⓐ Ⓑ Ⓒ Ⓓ			48	Ⓐ Ⓑ Ⓒ Ⓓ
35	Ⓐ Ⓑ Ⓒ Ⓓ			49	Ⓐ Ⓑ Ⓒ Ⓓ
				50	Ⓐ Ⓑ Ⓒ Ⓓ

/50

Post-test 解答用紙

Student ID	
フリガナ	
NAME 氏　名	

LISTENING SECTION

Part 1			Part 2			Part 3			Part 4		
No.	ANSWER A B C D		No.	ANSWER A B C		No.	ANSWER A B C D		No.	ANSWER A B C D	
1	Ⓐ Ⓑ Ⓒ Ⓓ		3	Ⓐ Ⓑ Ⓒ		11	Ⓐ Ⓑ Ⓒ Ⓓ		20	Ⓐ Ⓑ Ⓒ Ⓓ	
2	Ⓐ Ⓑ Ⓒ Ⓓ		4	Ⓐ Ⓑ Ⓒ		12	Ⓐ Ⓑ Ⓒ Ⓓ		21	Ⓐ Ⓑ Ⓒ Ⓓ	
			5	Ⓐ Ⓑ Ⓒ		13	Ⓐ Ⓑ Ⓒ Ⓓ		22	Ⓐ Ⓑ Ⓒ Ⓓ	
			6	Ⓐ Ⓑ Ⓒ		14	Ⓐ Ⓑ Ⓒ Ⓓ		23	Ⓐ Ⓑ Ⓒ Ⓓ	
			7	Ⓐ Ⓑ Ⓒ		15	Ⓐ Ⓑ Ⓒ Ⓓ		24	Ⓐ Ⓑ Ⓒ Ⓓ	
			8	Ⓐ Ⓑ Ⓒ		16	Ⓐ Ⓑ Ⓒ Ⓓ		25	Ⓐ Ⓑ Ⓒ Ⓓ	
			9	Ⓐ Ⓑ Ⓒ		17	Ⓐ Ⓑ Ⓒ Ⓓ				
			10	Ⓐ Ⓑ Ⓒ		18	Ⓐ Ⓑ Ⓒ Ⓓ				
						19	Ⓐ Ⓑ Ⓒ Ⓓ				

READING SECTION

Part 5			Part 6			Part 7		
No.	ANSWER A B C D		No.	ANSWER A B C D		No.	ANSWER A B C D	
26	Ⓐ Ⓑ Ⓒ Ⓓ		36	Ⓐ Ⓑ Ⓒ Ⓓ		40	Ⓐ Ⓑ Ⓒ Ⓓ	
27	Ⓐ Ⓑ Ⓒ Ⓓ		37	Ⓐ Ⓑ Ⓒ Ⓓ		41	Ⓐ Ⓑ Ⓒ Ⓓ	
28	Ⓐ Ⓑ Ⓒ Ⓓ		38	Ⓐ Ⓑ Ⓒ Ⓓ		42	Ⓐ Ⓑ Ⓒ Ⓓ	
29	Ⓐ Ⓑ Ⓒ Ⓓ		39	Ⓐ Ⓑ Ⓒ Ⓓ		43	Ⓐ Ⓑ Ⓒ Ⓓ	
30	Ⓐ Ⓑ Ⓒ Ⓓ					44	Ⓐ Ⓑ Ⓒ Ⓓ	
31	Ⓐ Ⓑ Ⓒ Ⓓ					45	Ⓐ Ⓑ Ⓒ Ⓓ	
32	Ⓐ Ⓑ Ⓒ Ⓓ					46	Ⓐ Ⓑ Ⓒ Ⓓ	
33	Ⓐ Ⓑ Ⓒ Ⓓ					47	Ⓐ Ⓑ Ⓒ Ⓓ	
34	Ⓐ Ⓑ Ⓒ Ⓓ					48	Ⓐ Ⓑ Ⓒ Ⓓ	
35	Ⓐ Ⓑ Ⓒ Ⓓ					49	Ⓐ Ⓑ Ⓒ Ⓓ	
						50	Ⓐ Ⓑ Ⓒ Ⓓ	

　　／50

|教師用音声 CD 有り（非売品）|

FAST PASS FOR THE TOEIC® L&R TEST <Revised Edition>
TOEIC® L&R スコアアップのコツ徹底マスター ＜改訂版＞

2019 年 1 月 20 日　初版発行
2025 年 1 月 20 日　第 6 刷

著　　者　　上仲律子、是近成子
発 行 者　　松村達生
発 行 所　　センゲージ ラーニング株式会社
　　　　　　〒102-0073　東京都千代田区九段北 1-11-11　第 2 フナトビル 5 階
　　　　　　電話　03-3511-4392
　　　　　　FAX　03-3511-4391
　　　　　　e-mail: eltjapan@cengage.com
　　　　　　copyright © 2019 センゲージ ラーニング株式会社

装　　丁　　森村直美
組　　版　　榊デザインオフィス
編 集 協 力　　WIT HOUSE（ウィット ハウス）
印刷・製本　　錦明印刷株式会社

ISBN 978-4-86312-350-2

もし落丁、乱丁、その他不良品がありましたら、お取り替えいたします。
本書の全部または一部を無断で複写（コピー）することは、著作権法上での例外を除き、禁じられていますのでご注意ください。